EMBRACING WOMEN

For my husband Edward Taylor
who needed this book,
for my family,
for every one who was part of this story
or is part of the ongoing story,
and for all who care about
the human aspects of ministry in the church

Embracing Women

MAKING HISTORY IN
THE CHURCH OF IRELAND

Ginnie Kennerley

the columba press

First published in 2008 by
the columba press
55A Spruce Avenue, Stillorgan Industrial Park,
Blackrock, Co Dublin

Cover by Bill Bolger
Cover picture: The author and Fr Romuald Dodd OP embrace after her
ordination to the priesthood in October 1990. *photo © Irish Times*
Origination by The Columba Press
Printed in Ireland by Betaprint, Dublin

ISBN 978-1-85607-625-8

Table of Contents

Preface

THE ROAD TOWARDS THE ORDINATION OF WOMEN to the priesthood in the Church of Ireland was a long one, with many twists and turns on the way! This book, for which I am privileged to provide a Preface, tells of that journey.

Change in the life of the Church often appears slow and in Ireland we are often perceived to be very conservative. It is therefore all the more surprising that the Church of Ireland was first among the Anglican Provinces in these islands to ordain women as priests, and to permit women to be ordained as bishops. The legislation to permit women to be ordained to the episcopate has still not been completed and finally passed in England or Wales.

What is more important than any legislation is that the ministry of women has been accepted so widely in the Church of Ireland, and that negative experiences seem to be comparatively rare. The fact that no legislation was introduced to accommodate those opposed to the ordination of women may well have encouraged a gradual acceptance of a new situation. The formalising of dissent can so easily prevent the healing of differences.

Ginnie Kennerley has herself been a key part of the story of the development of the ministry of women in the priesthood, and it is encouraging that she has written the story of what has been one of the most significant changes in the life of the Church of Ireland emerging from the twentieth century. Her experiences as journalist, academic and parish priest – and the ups and downs of her personal journey – ensure that this account conveys something of the excitement of the story to be told.

✠ *John Dublin: Pentecost 2008*

Introduction

I HAD INTENDED this book to be a fairly straightforward account of the development of women's ordained ministry in the Church of Ireland. Having lived through the whole period of this development and been personally involved in it to the extent of being one of the first women ordained in the Church myself, I felt I was in a good position to give such an account 'from the inside' as it were.

Once I started writing, I found more of my own personal story than I had intended was pushing its way in. I had not set out to write autobiography, but to pay tribute to dedicated campaigners such as Daphne Wormell and the Revd Michael Kennedy and courageous initiators such as Archbishops John Ward Armstrong and Alan Buchanan who had carried the flag in the early days and could too easily be forgotten by the next generation. In particular I wanted the new generation of women clergy to know what they owed to the gentle approach and careful research accomplished by the Women's Ministry Group in the 1980s under Daphne Wormell's leadership, as well as to the expertise and skill in debate of Bishop John Neill, backed by the Select Committee on Women's Ordination appointed in 1988, and the prayerful chairmanship of Archbishop Robin Eames at the General Synods of 1989 and 1990.

Yet, page after page of plain fact and careful analysis, however worthy, do not make attractive reading for many people, and I wanted most especially the women and men of the rising generation to read the book and catch some of the atmosphere and the emotions of those early days and the sometimes difficult evolution of the acceptance that women clergy enjoy today. So I have allowed my own story to emerge, if only as an illustration to the wider picture, in the hope that it will engage the reader and make the historic developments in some way more accessible.

I am strongly aware that there are many equally interesting

personal stories to be told in this area; and that as well as the stories of the ordained women themselves, some compelling narratives may come from those who opposed the move and those who took many years to come through to acceptance. But another book would be needed to do justice to even a few of them. I hope it will appear one day.

It is now more than 30 years since the matter was first debated at the Church of Ireland General Synod in 1976, and nearly twenty years since our first women priests were ordained in 1990. We have learned a lot about ministry as a church in that time, much of it specifically through the challenges posed by the presence of women clergy; but there is a lot more change and development ahead. I hope this book may make some small contribution to the process.

Ginnie Kennerley, Dalkey, Petertide, 2008

CHAPTER ONE

Beginnings

'No Theological Objection!' – the General Synod of 1976;
Women's Ministry in the Church up to this time.

I WAS A JOURNALIST writing features for the *Sunday Press* at the time. I had barely ten years up in the country. Still uncomfortably 'English', unsure where I fitted in, with less peer support than I would have liked, I was inclined to accept the prevailing view of Protestants as West British, snobbish, and out of touch with the real Ireland. I did not want to be counted among them.

Yet for some reason in May 1976 I suggested to the editor that it might be interesting to go along to the Church of Ireland General Synod beside Christ Church Cathedral to see what went on there. Surprisingly, he agreed.

When I got there, Catherine McGuinness, whom I then knew only as the wife of journalist and broadcaster Proinsias MacAonghusa and a leading member of the Labour Party, was on her feet speaking in favour of the motion: 'That this House finds no theological objection to the ordination of women to the priesthood.' A little later, Archbishop Buchanan spoke in similar vein, urging the demands of justice and encouraging the vote in favour, which came soon after.

Although I had two uncles who were priests, one Roman Catholic and one Church of England, the idea seemed a little strange to me. But I was impressed that this church which was held of little account among the general population should be so forward-looking, so intelligent in debate, and so in tune with the times. 'This is your lot,' a voice spoke in my head. 'You should be in there among them, not taking cover and hoping every one thinks you're the same as themselves.'

I went back to the office, wrote a short news piece, and suggested to the editor that an interview with Archbishop Buchanan might be of interest. And so it turned out to be, for the article, when presented some ten days later, was carried over a full page of the *Sunday Press*, with the full treatment of a big portrait photo and several highlighted quotations, and the banner headline: 'WE'RE BOTH CATHOLIC AND PROTESTANT'. My speciality as interviewer of senior churchmen had begun.

So too, had my association with the Church of Ireland, though this took a little longer. With the 'You should be among them' voice still nagging in my head, I went along to the parish church in Dalkey on Sunday morning – and fled. Must have made a mistake! It was a low period in the fortunes of this parish, in which many parishioners had betaken themselves to neighbouring churches in search of inspiration and spiritual support. A subsequent Christmas Day visit to Glenageary did not leave me much more enthused. Hoping for something enlightening on the mystery of the incarnation, I found a young Gordon Linney entertaining the children with Christmas chat and stories.[1] So I reverted to my usual diet of ecumenical services, wherever they might be found, and Alanon meetings, which probably taught me as much about Christian faith, hope and charity as any sermon.

But what was going on in the Church of Ireland at this time? Basically, the debate, and the pressure, was hotting up.

In the North, Irene McCutcheon, already a church worker of considerable experience, was impatient to be ordained. She had already worked as a recognised lay minister in England for a number of years, after an approved course of training, and felt strongly called to minister in her home area of the Church of Ireland. The administration of the Church of Ireland clearly took her claim seriously, since she was appointed as a member of the first Select Committee on Women's Priesthood in 1977, under the chairmanship of the then Bishop of Cashel, Dr John Ward Armstrong.

In the South Daphne Wormell, one of the first women lay readers of Dublin Diocese commissioned in 1975 and wife of TCD Professor of Latin Donald Wormell, became convinced around this time of the importance of an equal ministry for women in the church and found she was one of a number of

---

1. Gordon Linney was later to have a distinguished ministry as Archdeacon of Dublin, on top of his parish responsibilities, from 1988 until his retirement in 2004.

like-minded clergy and influential laypeople. Among them were the Revd Horace McKinley, then curate of her parish of Taney, General Synod member Frank Luce, and the Revd Michael Kennedy of Armagh diocese, with whom she wrote a pamphlet arguing the case for women priests.[2] This was published by the APCK between the same covers as an essay from the opposing side, written by Bishop Walton Empey of Limerick and Dean John Paterson of Kildare.

This little 24-page booklet, priced just 40p, achieved considerable readership through being sent out as 'required reading' for the diocesan synods of 1979, which voted strongly in favour of women's ordination, though not yet quite by the requisite two-thirds majority from the clergy. The publication played an important part in prompting informed discussion of the theological issues, which in retrospect seemed to have been somewhat glossed over in the initial General Synod debate.

To this day the summaries on either side are helpful. The 'pro' team set out to show that there was indeed no valid theological objection to the ordination of women, by enumerating the commonly held objections and then convincingly demolishing them: 'It's against the Bible'; 'Our Lord didn't choose women'; 'We have no authority to make this change'; 'It's against tradition'; 'A woman cannot represent Christ'; 'It would lead to confusion between the sexes'; 'It will make unity impossible'; 'It will split the church'. All these Michael Kennedy and Daphne Wormell showed, with respectable academic support, either to depend on a literalistic reading of particular verses of scripture or on the assumption that no innovation of any kind had ever occurred in the church of Christ. They concluded with this statement:

It is a fact that women are experiencing a vocation to the ministry. It

2. 'Should we have Women Priests?' Two Essays by Four Members of the Church of Ireland. Living Issues No 1, APCK 1979. The pamphlet was in fact the brain child of Gilbert Wilson, then Dean of Connor and soon to be Bishop of Kilmore, who himself wrote a number of useful books or booklets exploring the arguments for and against the ordination of women: *Should we have Women Deacons?* APCK 1984, *Why No Women Priests?* Churchman Publishing 1988, and *Towards accepting Women Priests,* APCK 1989.

is a fact that when they are ordained they have felt a great sense of fulfilment. It is a fact that the work of these women has already brought great blessing to the church. We in the Church of Ireland must provide an opportunity for women of similar quality to come forward and serve God and the people of God as priests.[3]

The opposing team queried the insistence on a 'contextual' way of reading the scriptures on the part of those in favour of women's ordination, also their claim of guidance by the Holy Spirit, their dismissal of anxieties regarding the negative effect on church unity talks, their alleged lack of serious theological exploration, their claim that Anglicans were entitled to lead the way for the universal church. Finally, they urged that the ordination of women would be a departure from the historic ministry of the church and should at the very least be delayed until such time as the churches with whom we share the threefold ministry of bishop, priest and deacon might come on side.

For the next number of years, until the legislation permitting women's ordination to the diaconate was finally approved by the General Synod in May 1984, these questions continued to be debated in private and in public, in church councils and occasionally in the press.

* * *

THIS DEBATE was not exactly a new one in the church. The Lambeth Conference of 1928 had already debated the ordination of women, and had agreed that while women could be ordained as deaconesses they were not 'ordered' as such, and would have none of the appurtenances or dignity of clergy. At most they might be considered an order *sui generis*. And already in 1978, the Lambeth Conference was to agree, following on recommendations from the Anglican Consultative Council, that provinces or national churches should feel free to proceed with women's ordination as and when they saw fit, as far as possible without impairing inter-provincial communion.

The recognition of women's *lay* ministry in the churches of the Reformation goes back, in fact, at least into the 18th century

---

3. At this point women had been ordained in the Anglican Communion as priests in Hong Kong (1971), Canada (1976), the USA (1976) and New Zealand (1977).

and the time of the Evangelical Revival, from which time women began to be involved both in foreign missions abroad and social work and evangelical activity at home.[4] And given our churches' emphasis on continuity with the practice of the early church, it has to be pointed out that women exercised a ministry of *diakonia* (service) in New Testament times, in the churches of the first and second century.[5] 'As I read my New Testament, the female diaconate is as definite an institution in the Apostolic Church as the male diaconate,' said Bishop Lightfoot in 1882, in his primary charge to the clergy of the Diocese of Durham.

Deaconesses retained a presence in the church probably for the first six centuries, after which they suffered a decline with the rise of the religious orders, since it was the convents that seemed to offer the optimum conditions for the regulation and protection of the ministry of women.

Although women's ministry in the churches of the Reformation began to develop once again from the mid-eighteenth century, it was initially confined to the 'para church' activities of caring for the sick and needy, especially women, teaching their children, and working as teachers, evangelists, nurses and administrators for missionary organisations. It was only in 1862 that the deaconess order as such was restored in England by Bishop Tait, chiefly in response to the need in the city slums caused by the industrial revolution.[6]

---

4. See David Hempton and Myrtle Hill, *Evangelical Protestantism in Ulster Society, 1740-1890,* pp 129-142 (London, 1992) and Sean Gill, *Women and the Church of England: From the Eighteenth Century to the Present* (London, 1994)

5. For instance, Phoebe the deacon of the church at Cenchreae, commended by Paul to the Romans in Rom 16:1-2; in the same list, Prisca, the wife of Aquila, both 'fellow workers' of Paul 'in Christ Jesus', Rom 16:3-4, followed by Mary, Tryphaena, Tryphosa and Persis, all of whom 'worked hard in the Lord'; and Euodia and Syntache, also named by Paul as 'fellow workers', Phil 4:2-3. There was also a clear tradition of women hosting in their own homes the eucharistic and teaching ministry of the church, two notable examples being Mary the mother of John Mark, Acts 12:12, and Chloe of 'Chloe's people', a local church mentioned in 1 Cor 1:11.

6. Gill, p 164 ff.

It took until the 1920s for the deaconesses' ministry to begin to move within the church building itself;[7] and even then it took until the 1970s, when women could be selected for training on a par with men, for the numbers to rise to a significant level, even though women knew the 'stained glass ceiling' would remain very low over their heads, barring them from any sacramental ministry.

This situation might have continued much longer, had it not been for the 'provisional' or 'emergency' ordination to the priesthood in the diocese of Hong Kong of Florence Li Tim Oi during World War II, and its subsequent effect on the churches of the Anglican Communion. Li Tim Oi had served for some time as a deaconess when she was ordained priest by Bishop Ronald Hall to serve the church on Macao, which had been cut off from the outside world by the war. The move was not well received by the other Anglican provinces, and Li Tim Oi renounced her priesthood when the emergency had passed, in 1946. But her priestly ministry had been effective and the genie was out of the bottle, as it were. Only one year later, the Synod of the Chinese Church wrote to ask the 1948 Lambeth Conference[8] to consider the ordination of deaconesses as priests for a trial period of twenty years.

The appeal was not successful, but the pressure was to be renewed at the Conference of 1968, by which time women's ordination had gone forward in a number of Protestant churches and was at least under discussion in the major denominations affiliated to the World Council of Churches. This time, confronted by the advice from its preparatory committee that there was 'no conclusive theological reason' against the ordination of women, the Lambeth Conference passed a resolution asking 'every national and regional church to give careful study to the question of the ordination of women to the priesthood and to report

---

7. For details see Gill pp 217-220.
8. The Lambeth Conference is the decennial conference hosted by the Archbishop of Canterbury for all the bishops of the Anglican Communion. It is not a legislative body as such, but its resolutions are respected by all the autonomous churches of the Communion.

its findings to the Anglican Consultative Council, which will make them generally available to the Anglican Communion'.[9]

When the Council held its first meeting in March 1971 in Limuru, Kenya, the Diocese of Hong Kong was in the front line once again. Its Bishop, Gilbert Baker, informed the Council that his Diocesan Synod had voted in favour of women's priesthood, and he had two candidates waiting. Would the ACC support him in ordaining them?

The Council was somewhat ill-prepared for the question, as none of the replies from its member churches had come in; yet the question could not be deferred. The answer was definitive for the Anglican Communion, being permissive but not prescriptive. The Church of Ireland received honourable mention in the reporting of the event, its delegates Bishop John Ward Armstrong and the Hon David Bleakley both having supported Hong Kong's case effectively. In effect the ACC advised not only that Hong Kong could go ahead, but that each Province of the Communion should make its own decision on the matter in its own time, and that all member churches were encouraged to respect each other's practice in the matter.[10] As a result, the first official women priests of the Anglican Communion, Jane Hwang and Joyce Bennett, were ordained on Advent Sunday 1971 by Bishop Baker of Hong Kong.

The next meeting of the ACC, as it happened, was held in Dublin in 1973, and this fact alone must have been an element in

---

9. The Anglican Consultative Council, meeting every three years, was set up at the same 1968 Conference to facilitate consultation between the churches of the Anglican Communion. Its membership includes lay as well as clerical delegates from each church, resulting in a certain freshness of approach.

10. Acting on a request from the Lambeth Conference of 1968, the meeting of the Anglican Consultative Council in Limuru, Kenya, in 1971, declared in Resolution 28 b): 'This Council advises the Bishop of Hong Kong, acting with the approval of his Synod, and any other Bishop of the Anglican Communion acting with the approval of his Province, that if he decides to ordain women to the priesthood, his action will be acceptable to this Council, and that this Council will use its good offices to encourage all Provinces of the Anglican Communion to continue in communion with these dioceses.' The Resolution was passed by a narrow margin, 24 votes to 22, but it was enough to launch a new era in the ministry of the Anglican Communion.

Archbishop Buchanan's decision to promote women's ordination at the General Synod five years later. The demand for the
opinion of the churches on women's priesthood was pressed
once again at the meeting and reported in church newspapers –
many churches had already responded to the call[11] – and as a result the Standing Committee of the Church of Ireland issued a
request to the House of Bishops urgently to consider the question of women priests, at the request of the Secretary General of
the ACC. The question appeared on the House of Bishops' agenda
in June 1975, when they agreed unanimously that they saw no
theological objection to the ordination of women to the priesthood. And so, without further ado, we come to the momentous
first decision of the Church of Ireland: 'That this House finds no
theological objection to the ordination of women to the priesthood.' This decision was underlined by the Lambeth Conference
of 1978, mentioned above, which declared 'the legal right of
each church to make its own decision about the appropriateness
of admitting women to Holy Orders'.[12] Already three important
churches of the Anglican Communion had done so, and had ordained their first women priests. After the Hong Kong ordinations of 1971, the Episcopal Church of the USA had witnessed
the irregular ordination of 'the Philadelphia eleven' in 1974, two
years before the necessary legislation was passed by the General
Convention. Regular ordinations followed in Canada in 1976
and in the USA and New Zealand in 1977.

There were other, more local, elements behind the decision in
the Synod Hall, of course. Subsequent to the Report of a General
Synod Sub-Committee on Women's Church Ministry set up in
1969, women had been admitted to the office of Reader, which
meant that they could conduct services of Morning or Evening
Prayer, the former being often the major weekly service of a
parish church, and could also preach. The first two women readers were commissioned by the Bishop of Clogher, R. C. P. Hanson,
in 1972, followed by five in Dublin Diocese, trained personally
by Archbishop Buchanan and commissioned by him in

11. *Partners in Mission*, ACC Second Meeting, Dublin 1973, SPCK, pp
40-41.
12. Lambeth Conference 1978, Resolution 21, passed by 316 votes to 37,
with 7 abstentions.

November 1975. There is no doubt that their dignity and competence in the sanctuary and the pulpit brought a new sense of completion and balance to the conduct of worship in the churches where they ministered.[13] They demonstrated that women could lead worship in an inspiring and authoritative manner.

* * *

IN THE SECULAR WORLD ALSO, women's competence in a wide variety of fields was by this time well recognised as being on a par with men's. For generations, women's educational opportunities and achievements had been no different from men's, so that already in the 1960s, there was nothing extraordinary about having a woman doctor, a woman bank manager, a woman barrister or solicitor, or indeed a woman prime minister.[14] In Ireland, the Woman's Political Association had made considerable progress in getting women elected to parliamentary and local council positions and the first woman cabinet minister, Maire Geoghegan-Quinn, was appointed in 1979, after an apprenticeship as a Parliamentary Secretary and a Minister of State.

It has been suggested by detractors of the women's ministry movement that the church was unduly influenced by secular feminism. I don't believe this to be the case; but it is certainly true that most lay members of the Church of Ireland found it increasingly illogical to continue to bar women from full involvement in the ordained ministry, when their abilities in church as well as secular life were increasingly being shown to be remarkable.

The Presbyterian Church in Ireland led the way with the ordination of Ruth Patterson in 1976, the very year of the General Synod vote which drew me into the life of the Church of Ireland. By 1986, seven women had been ordained for that church, and

---

13. The women readers commissioned in Dublin in 1975 were Daphne Wormell (who is to feature strongly in following pages as Chair of the Women's Ministry Group in the Church of Ireland), Patricia Hastings-Hardy (secretary to several Archbishops of Dublin in succession), Audrey Smith, Thea Boyle and Joan Rufli. All had a distinguished ministry, and Thea Boyle is still serving in the diocese in 2008.
14. Sirimavo Bandaranaike (1956 -59) in Sri Lanka, Indira Gandhi (1966-77) in India, and Golda Meir (1969-74) in Israel, had all demonstrated strong leadership abilities.

the Methodist Church in Ireland was moving in the same direction, with the ordination of Ellen Whalley and Liz Hewitt leading the way in the late 1970s. It was to be 1990 before women were admitted fully and on a par with men to the ministry of the Church of Ireland. The story of how that came about, and of how it looked and felt from where I stood, will be the story of the ensuing pages.

CHAPTER TWO

'Deacons Only!'

Ecumenism and Illness; Church politics and church affiliation

OR A FEW YEARS after the 1976 vote, I let my concern with Church of Ireland affairs slip away. I had other things to concentrate on. My husband, whose work as a director/producer at RTÉ was much admired but chronically insecure, needed a lot of support; and we were never free of financial worries. It was a time, though, when my exploration of Christian spirituality was deepening, and I found myself more and more drawn to reading and writing in that area, although Sunday worship remained foreign to my lifestyle.

At any opportunity, I seemed to be interviewing church leaders or exploring other faith communities. I wrote about and made friends with the Buddhists in Inchicore and the Hari Krishna leadership in Templeogue. Archbishop Dermot Ryan received me two or three times, never promising more than half an hour, but invariably spending over an hour talking, and also giving me an autographed copy of the new *Code of Canon Law*. After one such excursion, I was told that the archbishop met a prominent woman member of his flock in Lourdes, where she ran up to him saying, 'Oh, Archbishop, we've been reading all about you in the *Sunday Press*!' to which His Grace responded, 'O yes; Ginnie Kennealy[1] wrote a very accurate account of our conversation. Of all the interviewers I have experienced, she is the one I would rely on to get what I say right. But mind you, I'm not sure that she's a Catholic.' Needless to say, I was delighted with that comment.

Another interview in those days was with Dr John Ward Armstrong, who had succeeded George Simms as Archbishop of Armagh. We didn't, that I recall, talk about women's ordin-

---

1. Ginnie Kennealy was my by-line at the *Sunday Press*, chosen because of many people's difficulty pronouncing Kennerley, without tripping over the 'r'.

ation, but rather about ecumenical difficulties and the murderous rift between Roman Catholic and Protestant at that time. Although both Dr Armstrong and his opposite number Tomás Ó Fiaich, whose cathedrals sat on hills facing each other in Armagh, were both favourably disposed to dialogue and friendly contact, and indeed indulged in it frequently, elements in the communities on both sides of the divide were passionately opposed to it. I was horrified to hear that any murmur of a meeting between clergy of different denominations would result in a quantity of poisonous and threatening phone calls to the See House, before the Armstrongs had their breakfast.

The awareness of the religious divide stayed with me and continued to challenge me. At my Alanon meetings, most of the members were Catholics, whose style of faith posed no problems to me. At work, most of my colleagues appeared to be of the majority religion, many of them 'lapsed'. The only alienating thing at the *Sunday Press* in my ten years there was a notice at the back door one time announcing a communal recitation of the rosary scheduled for a certain time and place, and the line, 'You will please the Mother of God by your attendance.' *Mother* of God? How could the Source and Creator of all that is, possibly be said to have a *mother*? Clearly I still had a lot to learn about traditional Catholic spirituality!

So it was that gradually I began to consider enrolling for part-time study at the Irish School of Ecumenics. I had covered one of the ISE's early conferences, on 'Mixed Marriages' for the *Press* and been impressed. Further, a close friend of my Catholic priest uncle, Dr Maeve McGrath, had confided that she was planning to do a diploma there and pointed out that I, too, would be able to fit the study around my working hours. Then there was my experience of the Pauline Circle, an ecumenical discussion group in South Dublin run by the Legion of Mary, which also pushed me in this direction. I discovered the group in 1981 and was invited to attend some meetings, where I greatly appreciated the civility and courtesy as well as the subject matter of the discussions. Surely this mutual respect between Christian churches needed to be fostered and promoted North and South?

The only other place I experienced this was when, again as a journalist, I went along to a Charismatic Renewal jamboree at the RDS. There I found Catholics and Protestants praying, singing and laying on hands together with an unreserved and joyful mutual acceptance that I was later to find on visits with friends to charismatic prayer groups in Dublin and elsewhere. But despite my admiration, even delight, I couldn't consider myself a member of that movement. So how could I, as a non-church-going 'Protestant', get myself into a position to make some contribution to religious reconciliation in my adopted country?

Around the turn of the year 1981-82, I went to consult the director of the ISE, Dr Robin Boyd, to ask about the formalities for enrolling. He told me all lectures would be on Mondays if I took the Diploma in Ecumenics as a part-time two-year course. I could choose to major in Inter-church Dialogue, Inter-faith Dialogue or Peace Studies, but whichever I chose I would study elements of them all. Although I was clearly literate, the School would require two essays on ecumenical subjects as a condition of acceptance for autumn 1982. I undertook to let him have them before June that year, and filled in the application form on which I noted my denomination as 'Christian', not wanting to commit myself to membership of any specific church at that time. Little did I know how drastically my life would change within the coming year.

My husband Peter had a nagging cough that winter which he seemed unable to shake off. He had been distinctly off colour when we attended the Cork Jazz Festival in early November and would have gone to the local doctor before Christmas – had not the doctor suddenly succumbed to a heart attack himself. I urged him to go to another doctor, either one of our former doctors who had become our close friends or the doctor at RTÉ. He kept promising to attend first one and then the other and never going to either. Eventually I twigged that he needed some one he did not know, unconnected with either his work or his social life. I consulted our doctor friend Maeve, who suggested a specialist in general medicine at the Adelaide Hospital called Dr Baker. Peter agreed at once to see him, but even so it was early May before he actually managed to do so.

By this time I was extremely worried, and kicking myself for not having sussed what was needed sooner. While Peter betook himself to the Adelaide, which was then near the city centre, I went, not to some café as was my wont, but to find a seat in the Carmelite Church off Grafton Street. There was a Mass in progress, and I knew I could not receive the sacrament; but I sat near the back and joined as best I could in the prayers. I prayed for Peter; I prayed for us both; I prayed that somehow I might receive the grace of the sacrament even though I could not appear to do so. When I left the church at the appointed time to find Maeve, probably in Bewley's Café nearby, I seemed to be in a cloud of blessing.

She did not have good news for me. Peter would need an operation; he had a 'mass' on one of his lungs and a 'shadow' on the other. He was to go to see a surgeon next week, and to take medication to deal with the shadow, and return for further X-rays until it was gone and the operation could proceed. It was more or less the news I had expected – but my cloud remained in place. Maeve was probably surprised at my calmness. I went home in something of a daze to hear Peter's version of events.

* * *

WHILE MY ATTENTION was consumed by these life-changing developments, the Church of Ireland had been making some degree of progress towards the ordination of women. In brief, a Select Committee had reported to the General Synod in 1979, where its lack of theological exploration was strongly criticised. The question of women's ordination was then referred to the diocesan synods, with a great deal of briefing material, including the APCK's *Should we have Women Priests?* pamphlet referred to in the last chapter. Over the autumn and winter of 1979-1980 all these synods had returned a favourable vote, which amounted altogether to 223 clergy in favour and 126 against (almost achieving the two thirds majority that would be required in General Synod) and 622 laity in favour with 160 against – a comfortable majority of almost 80%.

At the General Synod of May 1980 the motion 'to make provision for the introduction of a Bill in 1981 to permit the ordination of women as priests' failed by seven votes to achieve the two-thirds majority in the House of Clergy, though 77% of the laity were in favour. However, it was said that the prevailing atmosphere was one of caution rather than weighty opposition. People needed more time to think about all the issues, whether practical, theological or ecumenical.

Since then, caution had prevailed. To push towards priesthood for women all in one go was felt to be too divisive; so the Select Committee instead suggested to the 1981 General Synod that a Bill be introduced the following year to allow the ordination of women as deacons. This was accepted without serious opposition by very comfortable majorities.

Of all this I was blissfully unaware when, in the spring of 1982, I had much more pressing anxieties on my mind. And when it came to the upset at the May 1982 General Synod, where a dramatic turn of events was to bring the bill down, I was only concerned to meet on its periphery a new friend, a clergyman who I hoped would help me to help my husband.

This was the Revd Cecil Kerr of the Christian Renewal Centre in Rostrevor. On St Patrick's Day that year, to mark International Peace Day with an appropriate article, I had driven north to interview him about the contribution to reconciliation being made by the centre he had founded just eight years earlier. Not only were Protestants and Catholics living and working together in the community there, convicted 'men of violence' and poisonous sectarian die-hards were repenting and embracing their former opponents of the other side. Clearly the place was breaking through old boundaries and planting the seeds of peace for the future.

Speeding up through Co Louth, I had sensed that this could be an important project, with implications for my personal as well as my professional life. I prayed under my breath as I drove that I would be enabled not only to get material for a good article, but also find the courage to ask for something for myself.

And so it was to prove. Cecil Kerr was a charming and co-operative interviewee. He was also pastorally sensitive and, after completing his story, he wanted to know something about my life. He listened quietly as I shared some of my anxieties about my husband's difficulties and his medical condition, made a few comments and comparisons, and then suggested that we have a cup of tea along with his wife Myrtle before I left, after which they would like to pray with me. While a touch apprehensive, I was very grateful, and had I not had the excuse of a slight cold, which enabled me to keep a handkerchief handy, I know I would have dissolved into a puddle on the carpet in front of them as they prayed.

This was my first experience of 'prayer with laying on of hands' and a more powerful way of helping some one in difficulties I could hardly imagine. Yet what intrigues me in retrospect is that part of me was dissatisfied with the prayer; for as well as praying for my husband, they prayed for my work as a journalist and what could be achieved through it. That already was not what I wanted. I was beginning to sense a call to be part of the ministry of the church.

As I met Cecil for coffee in Jury's Hotel in Ballsbridge, having rung him to report on Peter's bad diagnosis, I neither knew nor cared that the Bill to allow women's ordination as deacons in the Church of Ireland had once again failed to make it. All that mattered that day was Cecil's prayer for healing, courage and the presence of the Holy Spirit, delivered without embarrassment over the small table we shared in the coffee lounge.

* * *

L ATER I WAS TO HEAR that it was the Reverend John Neill who had scuppered the Bill. He had done so by pointing out that, while it was the intention of a church which had recently voted against women's ordination to the priesthood to admit them only to the diaconate, with no expectation of their progressing later to the priesthood, the ordination service, designed for male deacons who would be priested the following year, encouraged the understanding that women deacons would likewise in due course be priested, a development that would be in conflict with the intentions of the Synod. To the considerable embarrassment of the drafters, and to the fury of Irene McCutcheon and others anxious to see the Bill go through, it was withdrawn. The promise that a more carefully considered bill would be introduced 'free from all legal dilemma' within the next two to three years, did little to assuage their anger.

John Neill drew a lot of flak, both in and around the Synod and in the media over what was seen as last minute sabotage of the Bill by a man opposed to women's ordination. Reading the statement he made on the last day of the Synod, one can see that, according to his own lights, he had no alternative. Given that he was at that time neither on the Standing Committee of the Church nor on the Committee presenting the Bill 'to enable women to be ordained as deacons' he only had sight of the Bill to be proposed a couple of weeks before the Synod opened. On reading it, he realised that the implications of a permanent diaconate for women, which was what he then supported and planned to vote for, had not been followed through by those responsible for crossing the legal 't's and dotting the liturgical 'i's; and worse, that this constituted a legal impediment to a vote on the Bill as it stood. Taking advice from the honorary secretaries of the Synod, he delivered by hand a detailed submission outlining his observations to the General Synod office six full days before the Synod was to open, asking that the archbishop's assessor consider them immediately so that those proposing the Bill could be notified and take action to salvage something worth while and avoid unnecessary delay.

'I want to place on record my strong protest that given this notice, and no new factors being introduced at any stage since, it took until Tuesday lunchtime for anything decisive to be done,' he told the House. 'Our dirty linen was thoroughly washed in public, and people hurt in ways that could have been avoided by decisive action last week.'

Certainly it was not the Church of Ireland's finest hour.

* * *

AT THIS TIME, however, my only concern beyond Peter's illness and turning over articles at work was to get my essays written for the Irish School of Ecumenics. I chose two subjects, 'Charismatic Renewal and Ecumenism' and 'The Eucharist and Christian Unity'. Both promised some exciting exploration and I had little trouble getting down to them. A note in my diary for 21 January, '2.30pm H. McAdoo, See House', suggests that I had the cheek to go to the very top for help with the second subject. (As co-chairman of ARCIC, Archbishop McAdoo was even then bathing in general approbation that came in the wake of the September 1981 publication of that body's Final Report of its agreement on Ministry, The Eucharist and Authority.)

It was the first subject, though, which was to cause a further development of huge importance for me personally.

I had no difficulty writing about the charismatic renewal movement from the Roman Catholic side of things. Friends in Dalkey whom Peter and I had met in Tenerife some years before, Harry and Terry Murphy, were deeply involved in the movement, and would take me anywhere I needed to explore, introduce me to 'charismatic' priests, and tell me how their involvement had affected their lives. On the Anglican side, I could get a lot of help from the Kerrs; but I badly needed to find a Church of Ireland parish church that had been touched by this movement; and none of the few I knew qualified.

It was at the Pauline Circle that I found the answer. An Anglican member of that group, a Ballsbridge resident named Patricia Pearson, gave a talk there, probably in the March, about the Holy Spirit and her experience of baptism in the Holy Spirit. I was greatly intrigued and, knowing that she was an Anglican, I asked her where in the Church of Ireland this experience was to be found, and where I could find a Church of Ireland clergyman to interview about it. 'At Kill O' the Grange Church near Blackrock at the 7pm service,' she said. 'Just go along; or if you prefer, ring Billy Gibbons first and make an appointment to see him. He's in the phone book.'

I didn't do this immediately. For ten days in April, I was away on a long arranged working holiday in Rome and San Giovanni Rotondo in Calabria, exploring the Padre Pio cult with Irish devotee Mona Hanafin and visiting her friend Mgr John Magee, who was then Pope John Paul II's master of ceremonies in Rome.[2] How I felt justified in leaving Peter, still wavering about going to the doctor, I am not sure; but I recall that he was extremely difficult to live with at that time, to the extent that I sometimes needed to spend a few days away in the interests of self-preservation. In early May came the Dr Baker appointment and the frightening diagnosis; so it turned out to be 11 June before my diary read '9am. Billy Gibbons. opp. Shamrock Foods.'

2. Monsignor Magee was to be appointed Bishop of Cloyne in 1987, a long way to the south of his native Armagh, but at least back in Ireland.

I have long since lost the notes taken at that interview. I imagine Billy Gibbons told me about his own low point when he had been ready to give up the ministry, from which he was saved by a chance encounter with a visitor from the United States, a Pentecostalist through whom the Holy Spirit had come into his life in an unmistakable way. He must have told me about the difficulties of bringing spiritual renewal to a conventional Church of Ireland parish, where most people were perfectly happy as they were, thank you; about the dangers of splitting the community into 'old style' and 'new style' worshippers – something which had in fact more or less happened, with the 'charismatic' style worship confined largely to the evening service.

No doubt the interview was helpful for my essay, but what changed my relationship to the Church of Ireland and proved a turning point in my life was the worship at the 7 o'clock service that Sunday evening. I had feared upsetting Peter by going out to it, our habit being to spend Sunday evenings together with the television, but in the event he had no objection. 'Great!' he said. 'I can watch a cowboy movie!'

To me, the worship was simply amazing, a knockout. The words of the Holy Communion service were the same as in any other Church of Ireland church using the 'grey book' of the new rite, which two years later was to be formally published in the *Alternative Prayer Book 1984*. The experience was something else. From the first 'The Lord be with you', one felt this celebrant's delight in welcoming us to worship, his joy in being able to share God's all-encompassing love, the sincerity with which he spoke every word of the service. And then there was the music; not the old dragging hymns with a droning organ which I had learned to dislike at school, but a lively music group – violin, guitars, flute and drums leading tuneful songs on simple biblical themes. Most of all there was the heartfelt participation of the congregation, throwing in their own prayers during the time of intercession, greeting each other, and me, with affection at The Peace, singing their hearts out and even swaying a little to the music. I was bowled over; but even so, after one hour exactly, after the astonishing comradeship offered at The Peace, I fled for home, worried that too long an absence would disturb Peter's peace of mind. Increasingly he was a sick man, and the shadow on his second lung would only a short time later 'flower' into a second tumour, declaring his cancer inoperable.

Later that week, I went back to the little office opposite the church to see Billy Gibbons. Would it be all right, I enquired naïvely, if I started to attend church there, it not being my parish? Of course it would, Ginnie (in his lovely velvety voice). And would it be possible, even though I had never been confirmed, to receive communion? Yes, it would, though he would like me to consider being confirmed in the not too distant future.

Thus began my association with Kill O' the Grange, which was to continue until my ordination six years later. When I looked back at the end of the year, I could remember every single sermon Billy had preached from that first Sunday. I must have been very hungry indeed!

CHAPTER THREE

A New Parish Church

Learning to Pray – Losing Peter – Finding New Life

B Y THE END OF 1982 so much had changed. I had lost my husband. I had found a new family at Kill O' the Grange and at the ISE. I had slipped gratefully into a simple Christian spirituality in which friends prayed fluently with one another as the need arose. I continued my work as a journalist, but somehow my time expanded to include so much more.

At the end of the year I was to write:

Three wise men came to me this year.
The first said: 'You're a child of God.'
The second said: 'God loves you. He
has work for you to do.'
The third, in whom the light of God
was shining, said:
'Jesus loves you. And so do I.'
I thank you, Lord, for your love.
And for your messengers.

'You're on a cushion of prayer!' my new friend Liz Orr had told me at Peter's funeral on 22 October. Indeed, I had been on that cushion for some time. From the early days after Peter's diagnosis, friends had gathered with me on Tuesday afternoons to pray for him, first without his knowledge, later on with it. Regulars were Maeve McGrath, through whom I had first heard about the healing ministry in Ireland, our Dalkey charismatic friends Harry and Terry Murphy, sometimes with their son Paul, Robin Boyd of the ISE with his wife Frances, and Liz Orr, who seemed to be a sort of curate to Billy Gibbons.

My compulsion that summer was to get help for Peter. Early in the year, before his illness seemed more than a threat, I had gone with Maeve to a meeting at the Friends Meeting House in Eustace Street. I had spotted a name in the paper and rang her.

'That healer clergyman you were talking about, Stanley Baird, is talking at some charismatic meeting in town. Would you like to go?'

After the meeting, we joined the queue for a word with Stanley Baird, and Maeve, who on such occasions was a determined terrier, managed to carry him off with us for coffee in a crowded café next door. He told us all about his early days after being appointed to the healing ministry, very much the neophyte, when on one occasion he was asked to pray for a new born baby. He had laid hands on the baby in the incubator, prayed sincerely, and was somewhat surprised when the nurse in attendance had turned to the mother and said, 'There, my dear. Your baby will be all right now!' And when the mother had agreed, her eyes shining and brimming with tears, he had simply wished he had their confidence! Years later he had met the same nurse and recalled the episode. 'But didn't you see it?' she asked him. 'See what?' 'That wonderful golden light that filled the room when you prayed.' He confessed that he was somewhat peeved that God had not granted him the same vision, but reflected that the Lord doubtless knew best. Seeing what the women saw, at that stage of his ministry, might well have made him complacent. For the healing touch is God's alone, never ours, he pointed out.

We made a good connection that evening. Walking him to his car nearby I had said, 'It's all very inspiring; and wonderful to think that God can heal like this. But I don't think I'd ask him to heal just any little thing – like a pain in my big toe!' 'Why ever not?' was his response. 'You're a child of God!'

Well now I had more than a pain in my big toe in need of healing. When the news came through that Peter's cancer was inoperable, I had no hesitation in ringing Stanley Baird, even though by now he had left his specialist healing ministry to become rector of Drumcondra and North Strand, on Dublin's north side. He agreed to see Peter. Now all I had to do was get Peter to agree to see him.

'Of course I'll go,' was his response. 'If some one told me I'd get well if I stood on my head bollock-naked outside Dáil Éireann I'd do it! When does he want me to go?'

So one afternoon at the end of June Peter had headed off to

see Stanley, who asked him not about his sickness but about the story of his life. What was the first time he had experienced serious distress? And the second? After two or three hours they still had a distance to travel, so another appointment was made for next day. This time, I was asked to get off early from work and come along at the close of the session to the vestry of North Strand church where I found them still deep in conversation.

The ritual that followed was impressive. Stanley put on a blue cassock – blue for healing – and led us to the sanctuary steps of the church. Here Peter was asked to kneel, and I to stay beside him with a hand on his shoulder. For what seemed like about fifteen minutes, Stanley prayed Peter through every trauma of his life: 'Lord, there's a little boy here whose father has gone away. His mother has just left him with an aunt, and he doesn't know what's going to happen to him. But you are with him to look after him; you love him more than any mother can. Let him know that you are holding him, and that you will watch over him always.' It was incredibly moving, and when it ended, with a blessing and laying on of hands, mine as well as Stanley's, I was at a loss for words.

However, Peter got up, shook the clergyman's hand, thanked him, and we walked down to the door of the church, where he had left his car. 'Cor, mate! I'm glad that's over. My knees were killing me!' As good a way to return us to normal functioning as any, I suppose. And somehow I knew that Peter had not taken what happened lightly. The following weekend, when we were sitting with a beer overlooking the sea at the hotel down the road, the name of a man who was something of a *bête noir* of Peter's came up in conversation. I made a negative remark about him, as would normally be expected. The response was astonishing:

'Oh, I don't know. He's not such a bad chap really. I think he means well.'

I did a double take:

'Aidan? I thought you loathed the man! What's going on?'

A beat.

'I dunno. Since I spent that time with Stanley, I seem to have come over all tolerant!'

And he had. What's more, he never looked back. For the

months that were left him, there was never another poisonous remark about any one from him, whereas up to then these had been almost routine. What was more, the once hated Aidan became one of his most welcome and regular visitors when the time came for hospital. Peter became gentle, courteous and witty. The nurses in St Luke's adored him. If any one suggested to me, after his death, that the healing ministry had failed, I would emphatically contradict them. Peter had received the most important healing, the healing that continues into the hereafter. All the anger born of violence and neglect in his childhood had been drained from him by love. It was what I had been trying to do for all our married life, but the love of just one person had not been enough.

Stanley Baird's was not the only prayer, of course. Our Tuesday afternoon 'prayers and tea' continued and every Sunday evening, at Kill O' the Grange, someone prayed for Peter . Often it was Joan Howson, an elderly friend of my aunt's from Devon, who I was surprised to find in the congregation there. Sometimes it was Liz, or the person leading the intercessions. After a few weeks of this, I felt that I had to take responsibility, and at least occasionally be the one who offered the prayer. The first time I did so, my heart beat so ferociously as I gathered courage to take the plunge that I thought someone would notice. From then on, the extra vigorous heartbeat became the warning that something in me somehow was going to pray out loud!

Hesitantly at first, I found my place in the congregation: six rows from the front on the left hand side, facing the music group! I so appreciated their music and gradually became friends with many of them – especially Declan and Heather Smith and their son Ciaran, and Bert Van Embden, who played an instrument called an Appalachian dulcimer, made by his father, which was new to us all. The group also included Cecily West, later to be ordained, on the violin, an ultra pious Dutch lady, given to occasional prophetic utterance, called Dasha, and the group's director, Alex Curtis, who was also an organist of some renown.

Never having been a regular churchgoer, I didn't much like going to church on my own. Whenever I could, I'd enlist some one to come with me. Maeve McGrath came, Ida Grehan of the

Irish Times came; any one I could cajole came. Most of all I remember bringing Elizabeth Ferrar, an old friend through her missionary work of London friends of my family. A stalwart of St Bartholomew's Anglo-Catholic church in Ballsbridge and sister of the revered Divinity Hostel supremo the late Revd Michael Ferrar, it turned out that she knew the Gibbons family and was delighted to be invited. As time went by, Elizabeth and I found we shared a number of interests, ecumenics and India being the foremost; and Elizabeth as editor of *Search* published two of my Irish School of Ecumenics essays over the next couple of years.

It must have been just two months after I had become a regular worshipper at Kill that Peter, who had been given some experimental treatment as well as some radiotherapy, got suddenly weak and was told he needed a blood transfusion. Just the Sunday before, he had come with me to the evening service for the first and only time. Billy was away, but there was a wonderful sermon on the Prodigal Son delivered by Robin Armstrong, rector of Dún Laoghaire. Who was writing this script?

Days later, Peter was admitted to St Michael's Hospital in Dún Laoghaire, where he remained for several days. While he rallied, I feared that this pre-shadowed another nose-dive before long. And every one seemed to be on holiday: his consultant in St Luke's;[1] Billy Gibbons and his family; every one we really needed. What would I do without Billy? Could Peter die before he got to see him? Was it time to warn Peter's son Nicholas and his ex-wife Barbara in London? When would the Gibbons be back? I made an appointment to see Billy for early on the very first morning after their return.

The comfort of being able to pour out all my fears to him was enormous. His gentleness, his concern, the chaste kiss on the forehead, accepted as a sign of God's love, his heartfelt prayer, his promise to go to visit Peter very soon, all made me feel that somehow, he would lead me through all that lay ahead. Wiping my eyes, I heard myself saying: 'As soon as I get through all this, I just want to do what you do for other people.' I did, and in that sentence lay the core of my vocation.

Soon Peter was transferred to a private room in St Luke's. Before he left home, I heard him speaking to Barbara on the

---

1. The hospital in Rathgar, Dublin 6, specialising in cancer treatment.

phone. 'Yes, I've got cancer in both lungs; but I'm not going to die *yet*. I've a film to finish, apart from anything else.' He did indeed have a film to finish, a film on the life of Cyril Cusack, who ironically the film crew had thought might not live to see it broadcast. Not long after, the reporter/narrator Jack White had succumbed to a heart attack. Now it looked as though Peter too might precede his subject into the next world.

Visiting him one day in his pleasant room overlooking the gardens, mindful of what I had learned about the healing of past hurts, I broached the subject of a possible visit from Barbara, who had written him to say she would like to come. He turned his big blue eyes on me rather mournfully and said: 'Do you want me to die *at once*?' That was all he had to say; and I dutifully wrote her to say that he wasn't up to a visit from her just now; but maybe later it would be possible.

However, his son Nicholas did come several times in the course of that summer, sometimes along with his wife Bridget. And a picture of Peter and Nicholas on the balcony of the Dalkey Island Hotel from that time has remained on show in both our homes ever since. Nick found it very hard to accept the gravity of his father's illness, though, and it was hard to talk in anything but optimistic terms.

Peter himself found it hard, but not so hard that he did not go in one morning to his solicitor in Baggot Street to make his simple will: 'Everything to Ginnie.' Only once did he refer to the inevitable: 'If it comes to the ultimate, mate, please make sure I don't go out with a lot of nuns jabbering round the bed.'

I was determined that would not happen, but did my best to provide alternative spiritual help for him. I summoned all the assistance I could find. His old friend from RTÉ, Fr Rommie Dodd OP, went in to see him regularly, Stanley Baird went in, Paul Murphy my 'charismatic' friend went in, Cecil Kerr wrote that he was planning a visit, but most of all Billy Gibbons went in as often as he could and it was his visits Peter benefited from most. The only such helper he did not appreciate was the duty chaplain at the hospital. '[The chaplain] was here, with his prayer book and his platitudes,' Peter said to me one evening. 'I was as polite as I could be, but I *wished* he'd *went*!'

I tried to do my bit as well. Walking the dog at night, I would stop in the little seaside park near our home for up to twenty minutes at a time, and pray my heart out, my face awash with tears. As I did so, I was aware that the most crucial healing for Peter was spiritual healing. It would be no good returning to rude physical health if the bitterness and negativity that had been infecting his life were to return. But I was also aware that for him, physical healing seemed more urgent. Going through an old file from that time, I found the following lines I wrote for him.

> Hello, whoever you are up there.
> I'm told you can help me, even heal me.
> I'd like to believe that you can, that you will.
> Let me start by asking you something small.
> Please give me the strength, today, to do the things I need to do.
> Take away my illness, just a little bit, today,
> and make me believe that you can and will help me and heal me
> over the coming months …
> Thank you for the good things you have given me already,
> make me open to notice more and more of them;
> and please help me and be with me today.

> There, darling – just a small beginning for you.
> Please don't screw it into the waste-paper or reject it.
> It's the best I can give you today, in addition to my love,
> which you have always. X X X V.

For the most part, we maintained our optimism. Dr Healy told Peter that he was 'doing very well medically'. He even suggested that he could come home, 'at least for a while', around the middle of September. Peter started planning a final cut on the Cusack film and speculating on whether he could borrow a cutting bench to work at home. 'But before that, you should go and see Josephine. I'll be fine. You don't need to keep coming in twice a day now.'

Josephine was my stepmother in England, whose health had been giving serious cause for alarm, but who had also been giving me great support with thoughtful, prayerful letters all summer. Obediently, though with some anxiety as to how I was going to manage Peter at home, I booked my car on the ferry and took off early on a Thursday morning, to be back on Sunday evening. I can hardly believe that I went not only to Kidderminster for three nights but also to London for a day, to visit cousins who had been praying for us.

I returned to Dún Laoghaire just in time to head up to Kill O' the Grange for the start of the Sunday evening service. As I came in the door at the back of the church, I was greeted by Billy's joyous, 'The Lord be with you', from the altar. I was home.

But that very night in the hospital my husband, over confident and over considerate to the nurses, got out of bed to use the 'bottle', fell, and broke his collar bone. Now coming home was clearly out of the question. He was in pain. He couldn't move in the bed without three nurses to lift him. But he remained good-tempered and hopeful. 'This fall has set me back badly,' he said. 'But maybe I can still get the film cut before Christmas.' Five weeks later, just before his 57th birthday, he slipped into a coma from which he never really awoke.

Driving the now well worn route between Dalkey and Rathgar, I would pray the best I could. Long forgotten words from long forgotten services surfaced, and the BCP *Te Deum* was soon a favourite, whose cadences accompanied the twists and turns on the road. As Peter continued to deteriorate, I penned a poem for him, though I don't think I ever gave it to him:

> Beached on your bed like a whale on the sand,
> Ask God to help you and He will;
> Afraid, hurt and weak, just stretch out your hand,
> Ask God to heal you and He will.
> Aware of past sin, wanting life that is new,
> Just seek forgiveness, don't be bound.
> Christ is your shepherd; he's searching for you.
> One bleat from you, and you're found.

Looking back on those days, I marvel at what I managed to cram into them. Continuing to work four days a week at the *Sunday Press*, I called in at the hospital on my way to work and on the way home, and sometimes at lunchtime as well. In addition, I took part in the run-up to term-time studies at the ISE and began attending the Monday lectures, fortunately only five minutes drive from St Luke's. And I attended occasional weekday events at Kill O' the Grange, which was becoming my new family. On one such occasion, there was a visiting 'charismatic' pastor from the USA who embodied the less attractive traits of that branch of the church. Towards the end of the evening, he went round the circle of attenders, telling each one to ask him for a prayer – as though he could dispense spiritual or even material goodies on request. I remember I declined to do so preferring to seek prayer from those who knew me and my needs from somewhat deeper acquaintance.

My doctor, 'Tuffet' McWeeney, was pretty amazed at my energy too. Also at Peter's resilience. 'The staff at the hospital can't believe how well he's doing. They thought he'd go down quite quickly and he's actually improved. They think it's you who is buoying him up with that smile of yours and all your visits.' Earlier she had said to me, 'Virginia, he is *so* ill. Don't you think you should take a couple of months off work to spend time with him?' But I had rejected the idea. Peter would not want me sitting on the end of his bed all day, and to cry off work would have given him absolutely the wrong message.

But however I played it, the end was going to come. And in the heel of the hunt, I was just incredibly grateful that Peter died, as far as I could see, at peace. Billy did give me pause, the night he accompanied me to the hospital in the early hours for Peter's last, unconscious, minutes in this world. 'Ginnie, there's one thing I regret. Peter said to me not long ago that he didn't want fully to return to the church, "because of sin". I didn't know whether he meant *his* sin, or the church's teaching about sin, so I let it go. I should have explored it; I'm sorry.' But I was confident that the healing had been accomplished.

Around the time of his funeral, I wrote the following lines for Peter. Twenty-six years later, they bring me back to that time, and to the history of our difficult but always deeply faithful relationship.

> A million days, you promised,
> Our love would last –
> More than a lifetime, sure.
> But then,
> The demon jealousy leapt in to sear your spirit.
> Poison and scorn,
> Blows, brutishness, neglect
> Seemed to supplant your love.
> Yet still I knew

You loved me,
Needed my loving more,
Being always so unsure,
So fearful I might leave,
You dared me, urged me to go.
That way, the hurt would be less bad,
The fear fulfilled and finished.
Alone with anger you could find another,
To court her without fear, because uncaring.

But loving you, I loved your challenge, stayed;
And learned, little by little, year by year,
To tame your demons, gentling them
Like a blind lion-tamer,
Knowing always your love was what they masked,
Old hurt was what they sprang from.

And so at last they left you, and you told me,
'Our love will last a million days.'
I know it.

CHAPTER FOUR

New Commitments

New Bill at the General Synod; Visit to a New Country

B Y THE TIME 1983 dawned, I was already very active in Kill
O' the Grange. Billy Gibbons had lost no time enlisting me
to edit the Parish Newsletter. He followed this up by
inviting me, with my editor's hat, to join the Pastoral Council.
This was a group of parishioners, nominated by himself, representing the various 'departments' of the parish. They were seen
as an advisory and co-ordinating body to help him with matters
he considered too delicate or too 'spiritual' for the parish's Select
Vestry, the group of parishioners elected annually by their peers
to look after matters of finance, fabric and fund-raising.

We met at 7am every Saturday morning – a time at which no
one could easily plead other engagements. It being considered
both an honour and a responsibility to be involved, there was always a good attendance. Liz Orr was there in charge of Bible
Study groups, Tighe Taylor as co-ordinator of house groups;
Alex Curtis for the music group, Brian Kinch to advise on coun-
selling needs, the Sunday School superintendent, and so on.
Each meeting began with ten minutes of spontaneous prayer
and we usually continued until 9am. After that, as the one with
no family to go home to, I would sometimes be asked for breakfast at the rectory, where sooner or later Liz would arrive for further discussion on some problem or other.

By now I was also well established at the ISE, where for the
first time I attended the Methodist Covenant Service, in which
all students joined each January, under the leadership of the Rev
Robert Nelson, the Methodist patron of the School. I was greatly
impressed by the central prayer, which we said together:

I am no longer my own but yours.
Put me to what you will,
rank me with whom you will;

put me to doing,
put me to suffering;
let me be employed for you
or laid aside for you,
exalted for you
or brought low for you;
let me be full,
let me be empty,
let me have all things,
let me have nothing;
I freely and wholeheartedly yield all things
to your pleasure and disposal.
And now, glorious and blessed God,
Father, Son and Holy Spirit,
you are mine and I am yours.
So be it.
And the covenant now made on earth
let it be ratified in heaven. Amen.

One of the first friends I made there was a student from
Malawi, an Anglican priest and the son of a chief, who had enrolled for the MPhil course. I was amused that on all his books
he had written Bernard Malango MPhil, as though he had already received the coveted degree, for which I was not permitted to read, having no previous training in theology. Bernard
soon became a regular worshipper at Kill O' the Grange, where
Billy would often invite him to lead part of the service. We continued to hear from him for some time after he returned to his
country, but when he was raised to the episcopate in 1988 the
contact stopped. In due course he was to become Archbishop of
Central Africa. Another Anglican priest at the school, who also
became attached to Kill, was Monrelle Williams from Barbados,
who with his wife Heather was to become my lodger for a year
in Dalkey. But to the best of my recollection these were the only
two Anglicans in our regular classes, and there was certainly no
one from the Church of Ireland community in Dublin.

So since the director of the school and my personal supervisor,
Dr Robin Boyd, was a Presbyterian, most of the local students
were Roman Catholics, and I heard little at Kill O' the Grange
about the wider church, I was not too aware of what was going
on in the councils of the Church of Ireland.

But in fact the measures necessary for the ordination of women were being taken step by step. At the General Synod of May 1983 there were no more scenes of dissension and anger. This time the new Advisory Committee on women's ministry, the Standing Committee and the Legal Advisory Committee had truly got their act together, so that the proposal presented by Bishop Robin Eames to bring forward two Bills in 1984, one to allow the ordination of women to the diaconate and the other to permit consequent changes to the Ordinal (the Church of Ireland service of ordination) was accepted without debate.

At the time I was more interested in the idea of lay readership. Two Kill O' the Grange parishioners, Blair Halliday and Cecily West, were accepted that summer for study for lay readership, which meant that in a couple of years or so they would be licensed to conduct church services of Morning or Evening Prayer and to preach. This seemed to me as far as I could ever possibly want to go, so when I mooted the thought to Elizabeth Ferrar I was somewhat surprised when she said, ' Well that's all right I suppose if you want to *lay read*. But you know the Church of Ireland will be allowing women to be ordained as deacons soon. Why don't you think of that instead?'

And there I was, not even confirmed as yet. At Badminton, my easy-going boarding school in England, I had opted out of this rite of passage – the clergyman concerned being so uninspiring. Now I asked Billy if I should not at this point do something about it, as he had suggested the previous June. 'I'd forgotten all about it, Ginnie. But since you mention it …' So Blair Halliday and I were rather hastily prepared for the adult confirmations taking place that June in St Ann's Dawson Street. 'I have to say, I'm not too sure about the resurrection of the body,' I remember remarking at one of our sessions. I was not encouraged to pursue the problem, and the two of us, along with various other escapees, were solemnly confirmed by Archbishop Harry McAdoo. It was remarked at the time that our attendance the preceding week at the Church of Ireland Renewal Conference, led by Bishop David and Mary Pytches in UCD, seemed to have created rather more excitement.

But Harry McAdoo and I had something of a story ahead of us. Already I had encountered him in my preparations for the

ISE, cheekily asking advice about my essay on the eucharist, as well as interviewing him about the ARCIC Final Report for the *Sunday Press*. Around this time I came into his sights once again when Billy suggested that, with my background in broadcasting at the BBC, I could be helpful on the team putting together the Diocesan Council for Mission's *Know Your Faith* tapes. 'That sounds a good idea, Billy; but is she a member of the Church of Ireland?' 'As a matter of fact, Your Grace, you're confirming her in a couple of weeks' time.' Dr McAdoo was also to record a concluding interview to go with the *Know Your Faith* tapes with me, and when he retired to Dalkey some eighteen months later he was to become a regular visitor as he walked the Coliemore Road on his morning constitutionals: 'Just to make sure you're not overworking, child!'

Know Your Faith was a challenging project and one that I loved working on. My radio production skills, my new-found biblical knowledge, my enthusiasm for the life of the church, my enjoyment of writing, and my desire to get to know the clergy and leading lay people around me better, all contributed to the mix. I wrote the first talk in the series myself, basing it on the early chapters of the Acts of the Apostles, but baulked at delivering it. The recipients would expect words from experts, not parvenu nobodies; so I asked Declan Smith to take it on, as well as reading his own contribution on 'The Witness of the Church'. More prominent clergy we enlisted were Bishop George Simms (then already retired), Dean Tom Salmon, Gordon Linney, Stanley Baird, John Neill, Ken Clarke, Richard Clarke, Ricky Rountree, Bill Browne, Maurice Stewart, and Cosslett Quin, along with Billy Gibbons himself. Lay contributors included Liz Orr, Frank Luce, and Bet Aalen, then lecturing at Trinity College Dublin. Some of these worked with our subcommittee on checking the scripts for theological correctness – (Gordon Linney remarked that 'The Tapes' proved a good revision course for parish clergy). I was given the task of ensuring that the written scripts, when recorded, would work as discussion group fodder, and to make sure that the writers would deliver them in a convincing manner. Unfortunate speech mannerisms, parsonical voices, and too rapid a pace would not be conducive to good listening.

This meant that on Sunday mornings I used to turn up unannounced in one or other of the contributors' parish churches to check on their delivery. What cheek! But it was an educational experience for me, anyway, which mostly made me appreciate Kill O' the Grange all the more. One day in September that year, however, I had been asked to look after a visiting woman priest from the USA, Cynthia Bronson, and as she was accustomed to relatively 'high church' services I took her to St Bart's on Clyde Road, where John Neill was the incumbent. 'Hello, Ginnie. Doing a voice test?' he greeted me after the service – to my embarrassment, since I had had no thought of checking on *his* voice. 'Recognise bits in the sermon?' And indeed he had done me the compliment of using some of my *Know Your Faith* introductory talk in his address. That was really a big morale-boost!

All this time I was still working at the *Sunday Press*. One Saturday evening when I went up to 'the stone' where the hot metal was fitted into the frames for the next day's paper, two of the 'stone men', Sam Battle and Bob Robinson, embarrassed me with, 'Hello Ginnie. That's a great picture of you in the *Church Review*!' The colour probably drained from my face. I had never expected the two sides of my life to invade each other, least of all through a *Know your Faith* team picture in the *Review*. 'How on earth did you come across *that*?' 'We read it all the time, of course. We're in Finglas parish!' They weren't the last people in the *Press* to turn out to be members of the Church of Ireland. In my own *Sunday Press* environment, Dick Wilkes, the assistant editor, was one of us – a fact I only discovered at his funeral.

* * *

ON MY ANNUAL HOLIDAY from the paper that summer, I took a leap into the unknown and booked myself on a plane to Bombay and back. I had taken to Hindu-Christian dialogue under Robin Boyd's guidance like a duck to water, and planned to write my dissertation on how that dialogue worked out on the ground in India, both in the area of worship and in terms of ministry to the many Western 'hippies' wandering around India at that time. I was enthused by Bede Griffiths' books, *The Golden String* and *Return to the Centre*, and intrigued by his statement that he had gone to India 'to find the other half of my soul'; and I had further devoured Klaus

Klostermaier's *Hindu and Christian in Vrindaban* and Eric Sharpe's *Faith meets Faith*. Increasingly I felt drawn to investigate what spiritual meeting-point could be found between the faiths of East and West, perhaps because of the influence of my father's heterodox style of Christianity. (He considered himself an 'anthroposophist', as followers of the Austrian spiritual philosopher Rudolph Steiner still describe themselves.)

It was a big undertaking, but I was enormously helped by a young man called Michael O'Toole and the little handbook he had written on the Christian Ashrams of India. With his encouragement, I wrote not only to Bede Griffiths, but to ashrams in Bombay and Pune, Kerala and Goa, and even to a Bishop of the Uniate Church in Trivandrum, seeking accommodation, experience and conversations for my project. This was eventually presented under the title 'The Use of Hindu Scripture and Theological Concept in the Christian Liturgy in India' in May 1984, and subsequently published in *Studia Liturgica*.

In no way did I consider this expedition to be in the nature of any sort of missionary endeavour; but Billy Gibbons understood things differently, and held a sort of commissioning service at Kill to pray for my witness and my safety in a country where Christians were in general not appreciated and missionaries denied entry. As a result, I felt truly supported in prayer by my fellow parishioners at Kill, even if my purpose there was unclear to them, and whenever things became a little too challenging in India, I would remember them with gratitude.

The experience of Indian Christian spirituality in the ashrams was in many ways as much of a knockout as my introduction to Kill O' the Grange had been only a year before. Once again, the sincerity was manifest and moving, although the style of worship was completely different. It was best exemplified at Bede Griffiths' ashram of the Holy Trinity at Shantivanam, near Kulittalai, in the heart of South India.

There one was expected to enter the open-sided chapel at least fifteen minutes before the service began, to prostrate oneself and pray silently until the music and the chanting began. The more serious worshippers would already have spent half an hour or more in silent meditation on the banks of the Kauveri River, a few minutes walk away.

The eucharist was conducted in English, exactly according to the modern rite; but apart from that we were a million miles away from Western Christianity. All the music and the frequent chants were in the indigenous Indian mode with Indian instruments and with texts in Sanskrit or the local Tamil language. Every one sat on the ground, including the celebrant and his assistant, wearing Indian shawls instead of stoles. Instead of candles there were oil lamps, joss sticks instead of incense, and floral decoration laid flat on the very low altar or on the ground. Before the eucharist proper begins, there are readings from Indian scriptures and chants from the Upanishads, as well as psalms and Old Testament readings. The bread used for the eucharist is a large *chapatti*, broken for each communicant, who dips it in the chalice of sweet wine before consuming it and returning to his or her place for another deep and long prostration.

I think it was those prostrations that hit me hardest. The physical act of obeisance somehow promotes mental reverence, surrender and self-offering. But the entire meditative atmosphere together with the repetitive Indian music was deeply impressive – something I have only encountered in the West in the worship experience of Taizé, the interdenominational monastic settlement in south-east France.

There were ecumenical as well as liturgical lessons to be learned in India. Everywhere I went, it was expected that I would receive communion. And at the Christa Prem Seva Ashram in Pune I found that the community was itself inter-church, with sisters Sara and Brigitte, respectively Roman Catholic and Anglican, running the ashram in harness, inviting both Catholic and Protestant clergy to celebrate for them.

It was before the days of women's ordination for India too, but Sr Sara RSCJ and Sr Brigitte CVM, like their predecessor at CPS Sr Vandana, were powerful women, somewhat in the tradition of the Hindu *mataji* (revered mother). In Pune I also met and interviewed a secular women's leader named Shobhana Ranade, secretary of the Gandhi National Memorial Society, who was an enthusiastic campaigner for women's rights.

My short time in India showed me that such powerful role models, along with some campaigning, were necessary if women were to be enabled even to approach their full potential. Driving through the countryside near Trivandrum, at the southern tip of India with Fr Philip Neri, who had been explaining the work of his Christian Yoga Centre, I saw the slimmest of skinny-armed, sari-clad women, wielding pick-axes on the roadside, and carrying baskets of heavy stones on their heads. The men would not do such work, Fr Philip told me; they considered it beneath them.

The next day, I was on the plane to Cochin, on my way to the mountain-top ashram of Kurisumala, confident of a good reception, since Bishop Mar Ephraim had telephoned ahead to ask another priest, the novice master of the Order of the Imitation of Christ, to meet me at the airport and enable me to reach my destination. 'You will have no trouble recognising him,' the bishop told me. 'Like all the OIC fathers, he will be wearing a saffron-coloured soutane.'

Coming through Arrivals, I indeed spotted him at once and went up to him to introduce myself. 'Oh no, I'm sorry,' he said politely. 'I'm afraid I am waiting for *Mister* Kennerley.' 'I'm sorry, too,' I countered, 'but there is no Mr Kennerley. It's me. Look, here's the letter for you from the bishop.' After that, to Fr John Bosco's credit, he looked after me very well, except for one cultural problem. While he insisted on accompanying me all the way to Kurisumala, first by train and then by a hair-raising mountain bus 'to protect you', he refused to sit anywhere near me on either bus or train. It would not be acceptable for him to be seen sitting in the vicinity of a woman. Perhaps there was something personal about this as well, for he later asked my advice about whether it was a sin to experience 'certain involuntary movements of the body in prayer.' It was only much later that I twigged what his problem may have been.

However, in retrospect the most important lesson I learned in India concerned the power of prayer and the importance of personal contact. At the ashram in Goa, Fr Anand, the German Passionist priest who ran the ashram chiefly to help rehabilitate young people from the West who had come to grief through bad gurus or bad drugs, took me one day to the local hospital where he had calls to make. In the middle of an enormous ward of about a hundred beds, ten deep in both directions, I came across a teenage girl from England. Anand had told me that she had been abandoned by her boy-friend in a state of drug-induced psychosis, and no one could get anywhere with her.

With nothing to lose, I approached her bed and sat down on it.

'Hello. My name is Ginnie. I'm from England. Are you from there too?'

There seemed to be an immediate connection. A teeny smile and a shy look.

'Yes.'

'What is your name?'

'Carol.'

'Carol, you haven't been very well. Do your family know you're here?'

'No.'

'I'll be going back to England soon. Would you like me to go and tell them where you are?'

A look of hope that hardly dare hope so much.

'Could you find my mother?'

'I could if you'd give me her name and address, or even the town where she lives. Here, I think I have some paper to write on.'

She took the paper and wrote 'Mummy' and an address in Accrington in Lancashire.

'It would be easier for me if you'd write down her full name, so I can find her in the phone book.'

Calmly she took the paper back and wrote 'Mrs' and her mother's surname.

'That's good. I'll phone her as soon as I get back. I'm going not far from there. Would you like us to have a prayer for you to get better and go home?'

'Yes please.'

So I took her hand, sitting beside her on the bed, and prayed for her healing, her protection, and her homecoming, with thanksgiving for her mother's love, and God's. As I did so, I was very aware that the parishioners at Kill were praying for me; it was almost as though their prayers were flowing out for this lost but lovely girl.

The sequel to this was that I did indeed reach her mother the first time I rang her number. She'd had no idea where Carol was and had been desperately anxious. The news I had wasn't good, but now she knew exactly where her daughter was. Two weeks later they rang to say that she had flown out to Goa and brought Carol home.

That Christmas I got a very special Christmas card from Carol. Inside it said, 'Jesus has healed me and I am well again.'

CHAPTER FIVE

'No Bra Burning Here!'

The Early Days of the Women's Ministry Group – Towards ordination

I T WAS ON 30 May 1984 that I first went to a meeting of St Brigid's Society, an ecumenical Christian women's group at Daphne Wormell's home in Shankill, south county Dublin. Once again, I had my journalist's hat on. My mission: to see what Daphne's guest from England, Deaconess Diana McClatchey, vice-moderator of England's Movement for the Ordination of Women (MOW) might have to say to the Irish situation.

A number of women from various backgrounds had turned up. One was Jane Galbraith, a young woman of the Church of Ireland who had felt called to the priesthood all her life, always to be slapped down and told this was something girls could not do. Another was Delma Sheridan, a Roman Catholic woman who was a recent graduate of the Irish School of Ecumenics, also with a strong interest in the possibility of women in the priest-hood of the universal church. Then there was Helen Lambe, a friend of Daphne's from Tipperary with a penchant for writing letters to the *Church of Ireland Gazette* and *The Irish Times*, and Hazel Tamplin from down the road as well as Frank Luce, a strong advocate of the ordination of women and a member of the local parish of Rathmichael.

Apprised of the fact that Church of Ireland regulations now allowed for the ordination of women as deacons, and that every one present was interested to consider how things might develop, and how best to speak and act to further the ordination of women also to the priesthood, Dr McClatchey had come to tell us how they had proceeded in MOW, and to help us to see our own way forward. She remarked, by way of introduction, that the Church of Ireland was now ahead of the Church of England, which still did not consider 'deaconesses' to be in holy orders, or permit them to be addressed as 'Reverend' or wear clerical dress.

Diana's style appealed to me at once, and before long she was to become a great friend and mentor to me. This is how I described her in a short piece for the *Church of Ireland Gazette*:

> She showed herself to be everything one feels a 'clergywoman' should be. Gentle and wise, strong but softly spoken, concerned for the women – and one man – who had come to meet her, but equally concerned for their effectiveness in the church of the future ... A firm advocate in England's General Synod of women's contribution to the ordained ministry, she is markedly un-strident and no one's idea of a women's libber.

Diana suggested that it would be good to invite some men to membership of the group, and to encourage all members to bone up on some serious biblical study regarding women's ministry and to be as active as possible in the lay ministry of their parishes. 'And of course you must form a branch of MOW!' she declared, and began to tell us how this should be done.

To this last suggestion I immediately felt a strong '*No!*' response, but as a supposedly impartial observer managed to keep this to myself until later I could talk with Daphne.

Working for a number of national newspapers, and with a husband in RTÉ, I had become aware of how alienating many people found the extremes of the Women's Liberation movement. Churches and religious people being inclined to greater conservatism than most, I was sure that the demonstrations and door-stepping tactics of MOW, if transferred to Ireland, would consign all legislation to allow the priesting of women to the distant future.

Fortunately Daphne agreed, and between us we decided that the best way forward would be to form a group that would be specifically a Church of Ireland one, which would include influential men as well as women, which rather than going out-and-out for women's priesthood would promote careful and informed consideration of all the biblical, theological, psychological and sociological matters which had bearing on the place of women in the ministry of the church. Moving the Church of Ireland towards the acceptance of women in the priesthood and indeed in the episcopate would certainly be our underlying aim; but the aim was to be pursued with serious study and sweet reasonableness. No one would be entitled to speak of us as 'viragoes' or a 'monstrous regiment of women'.

For the *Sunday Press* that week I wrote a top-of-the-page piece: *Who will the first women deacons be?* My betting, as far as I can remember, was on Jane Galbraith and Irene McCutcheon as well as Katharine Poulton, who was about to enter training in the Theological College. In the event Katharine Poulton was indeed to be the first in 1987. Jane Galbraith was to follow only in 1995, after some difficulty fitting her preparation for ordination around her family life. Little did I think then that it would be me who would be joint second, along with Kathleen Young, ordained the same day of 1988 in Dublin and Belfast respectively.

For indeed my ten years with *The Sunday Press* were fast drawing to a close. I had achieved my Diploma in Ecumenics at the ISE; I had been recommended by my rector for training as a diocesan lay reader (licensed to preach and to assist at communion). I was hungry for more theological exploration; and *The Irish Press* was offering good redundancy packages for a limited number of staff members who might wish to change course. I applied, and gained my freedom plus the then princely-seeming sum of £7,000.

Trinity College was my next step. I knew my Diploma in Ecumenics could have been an MPhil if only I had already had some theological training when I started. Could I please do a master's degree now? The Head of Department, Prof Sean Freyne, was away on sabbatical so it was Prof Andrew Mayes, the Old Testament supremo, who interviewed me in his stead. 'You could do an MPhil,' he conceded. 'But how much of a hurry are you in? I'd much rather see you lay the groundwork properly with a BA in Theology and Biblical Studies.' I made a face. 'I already have a BA. I really don't want to spend four full years studying for another.' Mayes responded that he saw no reason why I couldn't do the normally four-year degree in two years, given the theological work I had already done and my familiarity with ancient and modern language study and textual criticism. 'In two years? You're on!' was my response.

There was a rider to the agreement, of course. I had to bone up on the history of Israel and some basic Old and New Testament study over what remained of the summer. That was no trouble. Indeed it was a pleasure, and one that I was distracted from by nothing more than my attendance at Fr Matthew McGettrick's one week course on Christian Meditation at Avila in Donnybrook, where I made friends with a charming St Louis nun named Sr Dorothy and began a practice of meditation which helped me through many difficult years.

By the time the new academic year started in Trinity, St Brigid's Society was evolving into a specifically Church of Ireland group, though it would not formally become the Women's Ministry Group in the Church of Ireland (WMG for short) until November 1986. In the meantime, we were an informal group with Daphne as chairman and Jane Galbraith as secretary, Revd Michael Kennedy of Armagh as vice-chairman, and Mrs Desirée Wilson (recommended to us as an expert on pension and financial matters) as treasurer.

It was sad that we had to lose the group's original ecumenical dimension in the process, but in compensation we recruited several crucial male members of the group, as Diana McClatchey had suggested. Several years before, when still a member of Taney parish, Daphne had held a meeting in her home that could be considered an early prototype of the WMG, attended by Jane Galbraith, Joy Kleinstuber (another woman sensing a call to ministry) and the Revds Michael Kennedy and Albert Ogle, then still in Dublin as curate of St Bartholomew's in Dublin 4. Now, as well as calling on Michael and Frank Luce, she recruited Revd Horace McKinley, who had been the curate in Taney during her time there and a strong supporter, along with Revd Cecil Hyland in the neighbouring parish of Tullow. There was also support from the then archdeacon of Dublin, the Ven Roy Warke, and Canon Stanley Baird, soon to become director of ordinands for the diocese.

The group had to be referred to as 'in', not 'of', the Church of Ireland, the bishops decreed, because it was set up by individuals, not by the church itself. But they would recognise our existence and moreover would give us a member of the House of Bishops as a liaison person with themselves. The initial appointee was the Bishop of Cork, the Rt Revd Samuel Poyntz, a strong supporter of women's ordination; but before long he was to be succeeded in that role by Bishop John Neill, the former opponent of women's priesthood, who was appointed to Tuam in 1986 and by then was coming to a very different view of things.

A brief digression to hear his story may be of interest.

John Neill had spoken in favour of the motion at the General Synod of 1976 approving in principle the ordination of women to the priesthood; but by 1980 he had retreated to a much more conservative position, arguing that, while God was indeed calling women to ministry, we should not assume that it was to priestly ministry that they were being called. More exploration of the varieties of ministry within the church and further prayer and discussion was needed before the church proceeded to admit women to the historic ministry of the holy catholic and apostolic church, which we shared with the other churches which trace their ministry back to the first century. So he had been among those who voted against the opening of the priesthood to women in 1980, and as will be remembered it was he who had forced the withdrawal on legal grounds of the Bill to allow their ordination to the diaconate in 1982. Yet he had been party to the preparation of the new bill, passed in 1984, to allow the ordination of women as deacons (possibly permanent deacons) and by this time was actively reconsidering the question of women's priesthood. A few years later, at the Lambeth Conference of 1988, he was to draw cheers from Anglican women worldwide for his introduction of the debate in Canterbury on women's ordination. In the most crucial years for the WMG, he was an unfailing support and a helpful adviser.

The group's 'softly softly' approach was noticeable throughout its formative years of 1985 and 1986. Our first priority was to educate ourselves in the matter of biblical arguments and precedents regarding women's leadership and ordination. To this end, we ran a series of monthly study groups on weekday evenings in Trinity College, where by this time I was able to secure a seminar room in the arts block. For guidance we looked to such authors as Elisabeth Schüssler Fiorenza, Elisabeth Moltmann-Wendel, Letty M. Russell and Sara Maitland. We looked at the gospels, noting that the first missionary Jesus sent out was the Samaritan woman,[1] and that the first witness to the resurrection, and messenger to the disciples, was Mary of

---

1. John 4:29, 39.

Magdala.[2] We looked to the Old Testament and found there prophets such as Huldah[3] and leaders such as Deborah[4] who were women, and noted Isaiah's reference to God as a mother suckling her children.[5] We studied the Acts of the Apostles and noted that the eucharistic communities of the church in the early days met in houses where the hosts, and hence probably the distributors of the bread and wine, were women;[6] and that the same appeared to have been the case in Corinth[7] and Philippi, while one of Paul's envoys to Rome, recommended for special consideration, was Phoebe the deacon (Greek *diakonos*).[8] We looked at the 'negative' Pauline texts, and found that even though Paul declared that women 'must keep silent in the church'[9] he also decreed that they 'must not prophesy with their hair unveiled';[10] and we noticed also that the Greek wording suggested rather that women should not chatter in church. We found that the texts from the pastoral epistles (Timothy and Titus)[11] forbidding women to 'have authority' over men, were oddly worded, suggesting 'exercise domination' rather than simply to teach or to lead; and my New Testament studies led us to conclude that these epistles were not in any case strictly Pauline, being composed by a follower of Paul's of a subsequent generation, more anxious than his mentor to comply with the secular norms and customs of his time.

Much of our work was led by one member or another of our group, subjects not always being biblical but sometimes of an ecclesiological or historical nature, but occasionally we would invite an outside speaker. One of these was the Principal of the Theological College, Canon Jim Hartin, who delighted us with his general support and his thoughtful discussion of the training needs of women with small children and of the development of

---

2. John 20:17.
3. 2 Kings 22:14ff.
4. Judges 4:4ff.
5. Isaiah 49:15.
6. e.g. Acts 12:12.
7. 1 Cor 1:11, Phil 4:2.
8. Rom 16:1.
9. 1 Cor 14:34.
10. 1 Cor 11:5.
11. e.g. 1 Tim 2:12.

part-time ministries to suit them; but he disappointed us when, having brought with him the first and then only female theological student, Katharine Poulton, he allowed her no part in the proceedings but to read a collect from the *Book of Common Prayer*.

My involvement in these study groups was an extra stimulus to my more formal studies at this time – both as a 'mature' undergraduate in the Hebrew, Biblical Studies and Theology Department of TCD and as a trainee lay reader in the Diocese of Dublin. I had been accepted for the latter in the second half of 1984 after an interview with the warden of lay readers, Canon Sydney Laing, and the Archdeacon of Dublin, the Ven Roy Warke, at Zion Rectory in Rathgar. (Many years later, on being appointed warden of lay readers myself and inheriting the files, I found a note that I had been accepted only on the understanding that great care would be taken over my initial deployment!) The great thing about doing these two courses of study simultaneously was that the work for the Trinity degree could be used also as raw material for essays for my lay reading mentors, chiefly Edgar Swann, rector of Greystones and Canon Eric Despard of Lucan.

The Trinity setting was also ideal for the women's ministry group's over-riding project: the organisation and promotion of the Conference on Women's Ministry in the Church of Ireland of April 1986. In keeping with our decision to take a non-aggressive approach to women's ordination in general, we agreed that we needed a Conference in a central but neutral setting to explore the issues surrounding women's ministry without polarisation, lobbying or militancy of any kind. To this end, we decided that the discussion should centre not on whether our church should move to the ordination of women to the priesthood but rather on how it would deploy and make the best possible use of women as deacons, given that the first woman deacon would be due to enter parish ministry within the coming year. To this end we adopted as our motto for the Conference, 'Receive her in the Lord!', St Paul's injunction to the Romans regarding Phoebe the deacon of Cenchreae.[12]

We approached the Archbishop of Armagh, Dr John Ward

12. Romans 16:1.

Armstrong, for his approval of this initiative in August 1985 – I knew him both from my journalism work and through my membership of the Church of Ireland Renewal Conference Committee,[13] while Daphne had a long-standing acquaintance with him through various church circles. His support and enthusiasm for the project was unwavering, and it was a joy, so close to the time when he handed over the See of Armagh to his successor Robin Eames, to have him celebrate at the Conference's opening eucharist and to chair the first session, which was addressed by the then Primus of Scotland, the Rt Revd Alastair Haggart.

The proceedings of the Conference on Women's Ministry in the Church of Ireland,[14] edited by Sheila Wayman, can still be read in a slightly abbreviated version in the pamphlet we published later that year. It includes the address on Women's Ministry in the Anglican Communion, past present and future, by Dr Haggart; Diana McClatchey's paper on the Role of Women Deacons in the Church; the Rev Ruth Patterson's sharing of her own experience of being the first woman ordained in the Presbyterian Church in Ireland, and a summary of the panel discussion, 'How will we employ women deacons in the Church of Ireland?' in which the main speakers were Bishop Gordon McMullan, Irene (formerly McCutcheon) Templeton, Dean David Woodworth and Canon Hamilton Leckey, with Catherine McGuinness as chairman.

I will not attempt to summarise the papers or the discussion, because, interesting though these were, the overall effect of the occasion seemed to me to be something different. It lay in the recognition of women's ministry in the Church of Ireland as a crucial topic by people from all spheres of the life of the church. We had feared that only women might turn up. In fact a large number of Church of Ireland rectors and senior clergy stayed the full course, along with no less than four bishops; and there were thoughtful and distinguished lay men in attendance as well as women, some of them lecturers or professors of TCD.

What happened was that although the topic had been clearly

13. This was led by my friend and mentor Cecil Kerr and included my rector Billy Gibbons as a member.
14. Available from the Representative Church Body Library in Dublin.

defined as the ministry of women as deacons, many priests rose to say that they felt women could not, should not, be confined to the diaconate. If there was to be a distinctive 'permanent' diaconate, a ministry of service and pastoral care alone, it should be open to men as well as to women; but what the Church of Ireland was most going to need in the coming years was ordained clergy who had a sacramental ministry as well as a pastoral one. It would turn out to be a matter of being fair to clergy in charge of parishes, more than of being fair to women, one speaker pointed out. What use would a curate be who was indefinitely barred from celebrating communion, doing sick communions, pronouncing absolution to the dying and conducting weddings?

No formal conclusions were drawn at the end of the Conference. No votes were taken. But all of us involved in the planning felt that those in attendance had moved forward into a new reality where all things would be possible, and where in the short term, women would be encouraged to answer God's call to ministry as fully as the current situation allowed. As they did so, and proved effective in the diaconate, we hoped that the next step would follow naturally and without any bitterness or ill will from those who had been opposed.

Looking through the written record, one comment of Ruth Patterson's struck me, one that later on expressed my own feelings about being one of the first women ordained in our church. She said: 'One of the most difficult things I found was that there was a strong feeling that the whole question of the ordination of women in Ireland, whatever their denomination, was being judged on how one individual performed, or failed to perform.'

If I don't get this right, I was to say to myself many times in the early days, people will say that women can't do this job. It was to be a big responsibility for us 'early birds'.

The Trinity Conference certainly fostered general awareness and kick-started the momentum towards the full acceptance of women in the ministry of the Church of Ireland. It also made it imperative that our planning group formalise its existence and membership for the continuation of our work. So it was that the Women's Ministry Group in the Church of Ireland, already effectively in existence for the past two years, held its official inaugural meeting in the Theological College on 25 November 1986. I was asked to contribute a 'meditation', which has survived in my haphazard filing system and which I quote in part to indicate the spirit in which we tried to conduct our affairs:

> We chose that Ember Day reading (1 Peter 4:7-11) because it reminds us so clearly that all ministry, whether by women or men, clergy or lay, is the ministry of God; that only to the extent that we are close to God and inspired by the Holy Spirit can our speech or our actions be helpful to his people.
>
> We must be good stewards of God's varied grace, Peter says. In other words, we are to employ the Spirit's gifts to us, whether as preachers or prophets, teachers or counsellors, musicians, intercessors or channels of healing, not for our own personal satisfaction but for the building up of the Christian community, which is Christ's body. But there is no point in our doing so unless God's love for his people is overflowing in our hearts. So let us pray today that God will drench us with a new outpouring of his love, so that we may act as channels of that love to others.
>
> For women called to ministry ... we must pray also for courage to respond to God's call. Too many women fail to come forward for fear of rejection or ridicule, or through lack of self-confidence. Others remain estranged from the church on account of a past hurt for which the church as a whole is blamed. We need always to be on the lookout for such women, offering our encouragement and acceptance. That is perhaps the most important reason for our existence in this group.
>
> ... Let us pray for true humility, openness to [God's] Word, and a spirit of loving service to the One God, our loving creator, redeemer and sanctifier; who acts as both Father and Mother to us and who comes alongside us in Jesus Christ our Lord, in the power of the Holy Spirit.

Shortly after the Conference in Trinity which gave rise to this formalising of the WMG, my own time there had drawn to a close. Final examinations in May were gruelling enough and I knew there was one paper in which, due to sheer tiredness, I did myself less than justice. I used to trail in to the campus each morning feeling amazed that people half my age were managing to party and conduct love affairs even as they too faced exams, whereas I did nothing but eat, sleep and revise. But in the heel of the hunt I emerged with First Class Honours, a morale boost which gave me the confidence seriously to consider for the first time the possibility of offering myself for ordination.

It was auxiliary ministry that seemed to me most suitable at that point. I was just about to launch on my work as a lay reader, conducting and preaching at services other than my own every Sunday morning, wearing the magenta garb and pale blue scarf originally designed by Daphne and Mrs Alan Buchanan for the first group of women readers in the diocese.[15] I had noticed over the past year how much of Billy Gibbons' time was taken up with administration and parish organisation and preferred to think of myself having the freedom to write and maybe to do some teaching, having seen how sparse was the provision of intelligent theology geared to non-specialists in the field.

This was the answer I gave to Canon Jim Hartin when, at the CACTM[16] interviews late in 1986 he asked me, 'But why can't I have you here all the time, to train for the stipendiary ministry?' There was also another problem: I did not like to think of myself having to take up residence in the Theological College along with dozens of students, most of whom would be in their early twenties. Apart from anything else, what would I do with the dog?

Fate was to have the last laugh on me here; but for the moment I escaped the Theological College, its prep school atmosphere, and its catering, and was prescribed a course of study that would 'fill in' the Anglican elements of liturgy, pastoralia and church history which had not been included in the degree course at Trinity. I was also invited to lecture the Church of Ireland ordinands and others in the department in TCD on St John's gospel, which had been the subject of my undergraduate thesis for Sean Freyne.

My association with the Theological College at this stage was useful for the work of the Women's Ministry Group. One of our major events of 1987 was what we called the 'Jean Mayland

---

15. After my Commissioning on 1.11.86, I was assigned to assist the Rev Wilbert Gourley in Finglas with St Georges and the Free Church, a good half hour's drive across the River Liffey from my home in Dalkey, and served there mostly alongside the Revd Bill Wilkinson, a late vocation auxiliary priest of Dublin diocese.

16. The Church's Advisory Committee on Training for Ministry

Seminar', held in the college on Saturday 5 June, at which the cases for and against women's ordination were skilfully presented by our guest.[17] The day attracted some thirty women and a couple of men and was devoted largely to lay ministry in the morning and ordained ministry in the afternoon.

Mayland's key points regarding women's ordination are worth recording. First considering the 'case against', she explored the three most common arguments:

> 1) The 'ecumenical' argument of those anxious about relations with the Roman Catholic and Orthodox churches. She regretted that this should matter more to people than the internal unity of the Anglican Communion, or for that matter our relations with Lutheran, Reformed and Methodist churches already ordaining women. She also pointed out that in all of church history, no development had ever occurred uniformly in all Christian communities.
>
> 2) The 'icon of Christ' fallacy, developed under the influence of Orthodox churches, implying that female humanity is not redeemed. Priests may indeed be considered representatives but certainly not representations of Christ.
>
> 3) The 'headship' argument, holding that women are constitutionally unsuitable for leadership, as well as being biblically 'forbidden' to 'hold authority over men'. Over-simplistic sexual stereotyping is not in accordance with the facts, she said, although she would like to see new models of shared leadership developed for men and women alike.

Coming to the 'Case For', Jean Mayland shared the three reasons for women's ordination which she found most cogent:

> 1) Women are being called to ordained ministry and their ministry as priests is already recognised in many places.
>
> 2) The priesthood should represent the whole of the community before God, and the whole of God before the community. The feminine in both God and the community is a value which the church needs.

---

17. Jean Mayland was at that point the President of the Ecumenical Forum of European Christian Women, a lecturer in the Church of England's Northern Ordination Course, a member of the British Council of Churches and a lay reader in York Minster, where her husband Ralph Mayland was a residentiary canon. She was subsequently ordained to the priesthood in the Church of England.

3) The mission of the church requires it, in a society which affirms the dignity and the full humanity of women.

This was an important event in the development of the WMG, which came at just the right time to inspire and inform our activity in the three crucial years to come, which would see the ordination of women first as deacons, starting with Katharine Poulton later that month on 23 June, and then as priests in 1990.

CHAPTER SIX

Ordination to the Diaconate

Sexuality in the Church; a Surprise Appointment

OUR CONCERN IN THE Women's Ministry Group was not all with argumentation and tactics. Whether at committee meetings, on social occasions, or one to one, we talked and teased out our ideas on sexuality, spirituality, complementarity and anthropology.

We did not always agree! While Daphne tended to urge that the church needed women to bring a feminine perspective and female sensitivity to its ministry, I would grow impatient at the general assumption of a gulf between male and female humanity. It would infuriate me when well-meaning male supporters would tell us that the church needed 'your feminine intuition and gentleness', as though all women were basically brainless but could make up for male harshness by exuding motherliness down the aisle and in the sick-room.

As the firstborn of two girls in our family, carrying the expectations of academic distinction from the previous generation, it had never occurred to me that female brains might be less acute than male ones, or that women lacked anything but brawn in the war of the sexes. Long before my vocation to the priesthood became apparent, I was affronted by the conservatives' implication that women were somehow not fully human, that ordination as priests would be ineffective in their case, that the special character of priesthood simply would not 'stick' to them, but rather would fall from their being like water from a duck's back.

In my studies at Trinity, I had found that the Jewish tradition tended to see women as 'other', perhaps frighteningly so, and that the Christian Church had inherited this attitude. But we had to insist on the fact that women are indeed fully human and to be seen as created equally with men in God's likeness, for according to the inspiration of Genesis 1, 'God created humankind in his image ... male and female created he them'.[1] Thus a priest-hood that represented only the male side of humanity – and in-deed the male side of God – was chronically deficient and in-complete.

The model for sexual differentiation I had in my head, there-fore, was of a continuum – a straight line with the very male at one end and the very female at the other, with the more bal-anced (or indeed indeterminate) somewhere in the middle. At boarding school in England a teacher had remarked of me that 'Ginnie is extraordinary; she is so very feminine but she has a male mind!' I had taken this as a compliment, even if it was something of an exaggeration, and my friends at university and throughout my life had always been people somewhere in the middle of the continuum. Neither fluffy blondes nor muscle-bound rowing blues appealed to me at all. Similarly all my jobs in adult life had been ones equally aspired to by men – as a uni-versity lecturer, a BBC director, and a journalist. And as I con-templated the gifts of the then exclusively male clergy of the Church of Ireland, and indeed of the Roman Catholic Church in Ireland, I noticed that those who were most appreciated by their parishioners had a well developed feminine side to their charac-ters.

So in the WMG I argued that the case for women in the priesthood should be presented not so much as offering the church the unique talents and qualities of women, as of alerting it that for nearly 2000 years it had been starving itself of the gifts of one half of humanity. We all agreed also that no one, whether male or female, has a right to be ordained; but all equally should have the right to have their vocation tested by the church, that is, to be considered for ordination training by a selection committee and possibly selected for ordination by a bishop of the church.

By this time it was clear that many women had already given up on the church. Feminist theologicans such as Mary Daly and Daphne Hampson saw it as irretrievably patriarchal and de-fined themselves as 'post-Christian'. Women called to priest-hood such as Suzanne Fageol in England had formed their own breakaway groups where they could celebrate the sacraments with their sisters in defiance of episcopal and synodical authority.

1. Genesis 1:27.

Other women around the world were becoming aggressively impatient. In the USA this had lead to the 'irregular' ordination of eleven women in Philadelphia on 29 July 1974, more than two years before ECUSA's General Convention agreed to women's ordination by a tiny majority in September 1976. In England and Australia impatience had boiled over in alienating demonstrations and heckling, although for the most part decorum was maintained.

As mentioned earlier, we felt that any show of impatience would be counterproductive in our case, and we were fortunate that in Ireland there simply was not the head of steam built up by years of frustration that women in England had experienced. But we kept in touch with what was going on elsewhere, largely through Daphne's contacts and the Women's Ministry publications[2] she subscribed to, and occasionally we welcomed visiting women priests from other churches of the Anglican Communion.

One such was the Revd Alice Medcof, who was already running her own parish in Canada; another was the Revd Noreen Mooney, a deacon from Long Island; another, the Revd Diane Miller-Keely of New Zealand, studying at the ISE, who not only worked alongside her husband Bruce but was archdeacon for a group of parishes in Auckland diocese; and another, the distinguished Dr Patricia Wilson-Kastner, lecturer in homiletics at General Theological Seminary in New York City, who the Archbishop of Dublin asked me to look after on her visit to Dublin as a member of the worldwide Methodist Anglican Consultations. None of these women at that time were entitled to celebrate the sacraments in the Church of Ireland – a bar which we challenged, arguing that if people could experience the ministry of a woman priest, even once, it would help them to make up their minds when the time to vote came. Our bishops' ruling, understandable in view of the Anglican principle that all should respect each other's rules when in a province not their own, was that they could robe and officiate only as deacons, this being the only ministry to which women in the Church of Ireland were then admitted.

In those early days, when the question of priesthood for

---

2. Chiefly ECUSA's *Journal of Women's Ministries*.

women was still in the balance and acceptance of women clergy in general remained uncertain, there were not many women in Ireland who ventured to offer themselves for the ordained ministry. The female lay readers, the first of whom were commissioned in 1972 in Clogher and in 1975 in Dublin, had already shown that women could lead worship and preach as well as any man, and it was an unfortunate fact that in terms of the worship of the church, deacons were not permitted any functions which were not equally open to lay readers. So it took someone with a clear vision of day-to-day pastoral ministry in a parish to offer for a ministry which might remain indefinitely 'second class', deacons being by definition denied both sacramental activity and parish leadership roles.

However, following on Katharine Poulton in 1984, Kathleen Young of Belfast, a widow with a background as a teacher of physiotherapy, had entered the Theological College as a full-time student in 1985 and Sheila Zietsman from Zimbabwe was to follow in 1987, having been commended to Bishop Walton Empey of Meath and Kildare diocese by the then Bishop of London, Graham Leonard.

Sheila had been hoping to be ordained to the diaconate in London and had been doing some pastoral work for the Revd John Stott's famous church, All Souls in Langham Place, and for St John's Church, Marble Arch, but due to some immigration regulations ordination in England was not possible for her. Bishop Empey lit on Kill O' the Grange as a likely spiritual home for her, and so it was that the two of us met and became friends. Alhough she was housed with a young couple near to the parish church, Sheila spent a good deal of time at my home in Dalkey. The 'encouragment' work of the WMG thus became more specific for me, as Sheila and I compared our ideas of ministry, our attitudes to authority, and indeed our concepts of God, of salvation and of vocation. The fact that we were very different, Sheila majoring largely on 'judgement' in those days and I on 'grace', was an important reminder that, as with the world, it takes 'all sorts' to minister in the church.

In Kill O'the Grange, I was continuing my membership of the Pastoral Council and my attendance at the evening communion service, although Sunday mornings always saw me ministering in the St Georges and Finglas group in North Dublin. Sometimes I would preach at the evening service, sometimes I would lead prayers, and often I would be called by a last minute signal from Billy to assist with the chalice – such a privilege it was to offer fellow worshippers 'the blood of Christ'. Around this time we were also introduced as a parish to the healing ministry by a visit from the Bishop of Singapore, Chu Ban It, and one of his clergy Derek Hong.

It was a time when my friend and teacher, Liz Orr, herself a devoted counsellor to those suffering from depression, had become chronically depressed herself. A wounding remark from a parishioner, coming around the same time as a hysterectomy, had left her feeling chronically unworthy, so unworthy that when the time came for communion she would slip out of the church in tears to walk around outside until she could gather the composure to return. One evening I had followed her out to find her in this state and to put my arms around her saying, 'It is going to be all right. God will bring you through this. I know he will.'

It was Derek Hong who was instrumental in her healing. Kneeling beside her on the sanctuary step, my hand on her shoulder, I witnessed his stern reprimand to whatever demonic entity he believed to be oppressing her, banishing it in Christ's name from her presence. We never spoke of what had happened, but after that Liz replied to enquiries that she was, 'Much better, thank you, since Sunday evening.' And she was.

In the ensuing months, special healing time after the evening service once a month became a standard part of the programme. For some of us it proved somewhat exhausting, given that the healing team was required to meet for prayer an hour before the service and to continue ministering to individuals often up to 10.30pm. But people did experience healing, and it was an important demonstration of the importance of the healing ministry of the church – an illustration, also, of what lay people, whether women or men, could achieve through faithful prayer and openness to one another and to the Holy Spirit. Some female members of the healing team who had no thought of seeking ordination were among those most sought after by ailing or distressed members of the congregation in their need.

M Y OWN ORDINATION to the diaconate was fast approaching. My church history studies with Jim Hartin (mostly about Lambeth Conferences and the Anglican Consultative Council), my sessions with Canon Billy Marshall on philosophy of religion, and my attendance at Dr Maurice Stewart's liturgy lectures were completed; and on the pastoral front I had learned a great deal through attendance at the Westminster Pastoral Foundation in London's Kensington Square in the summer of 1986 and later at training groups in All Hallows, the Vincentian Seminary in North Dublin. Given my lecturing commitments in Trinity, which now included a course on the Book of Revelation and classes in New Testament Greek as well as the lectures on John's gospel, I was also involved with Theological College staff in examiners' meetings that spring and early summer and my diary is full of 'Correct Exam Papers' notes.

Amid all the activity in the college, with the WMG and the Forum for European Christian Women, and with the Glenstal Ecumenical Conference (of which more later) I was looking forward to the ordination ceremony with excitement and with not a little anxiety as to where Archbishop Caird would decide that I should 'serve my title'.[3] I was also worrying a little what seriously gainful employment I might find after four years' hand-to-mouth existence since leaving the *Sunday Press*.

In anticipation of the big day, Bill Wilkinson, my liturgical partner in St George's, Finglas and the Free Church, generously presented me with an elegant green stole and a white one to match, specifically for ordination day; my stepmother gave me the purple one required for the penitential seasons of Lent and Advent, while Kill O' the Grange parish gifted the red one, symbolic of the activity of the Holy Spirit and of martyrdom.

In due course I was summoned to the See House in Temple Road for an interview with the Archbishop. Donald Caird was known to me and to WMG members as being extremely cautious about women's ordination – he had told us as much at one of our meetings – but I knew him also to be a fair-minded man who would not ask anything unreasonable of me.

---

3. The phrase points to the requirement that all newly ordained deacons be attached to a specific parish for a minimum of two years training under an experienced rector.

'What would you say to Bray?' he enquired as soon as I was seated in his study. I was surprised but not displeased, having been told that he would probably send me to Whitechurch, where the rector was seriously overworked in a fast-growing suburban area at the foot of the Dublin Mountains. Bray I knew; indeed I had lived there for a couple of years in the late 1960s. His apparent enquiry was of course the announcement of his decision on my placement; so I responded equably that Bray would be both convenient and known to me, and asked should I call on the rector to make arrangements.

The rector was David Godfrey, a man of about my own age whom I had already met at the annual ecumenical 'Summerfest' conference in Corrymeela some years before. A couple of weeks after my meeting with the archbishop, he and his wife Heather gave me a warm welcome over a lunch of quiche and salad. He was greatly looking forward to some help, having run himself into the ground of late through overwork. He hoped I could do a good deal of visiting for him, as well as preaching and leading sections of the worship, and attend the parish prayer group which met each week, usually in a parishioner's home. He gave me a parish list, told me about a retired priest, Sam Allen, who also gave some help with services, and explained that he would have a special role in the ordination service in a few weeks time. I left rather wondering how much time I would find for the writing I had promised myself I would return to, or for my occasional lectures in TCD; and I had to face the fact that Kill O' the Grange evening services, my spiritual sustenance for the past six years, would soon be a thing of the past.

So far, so routine; but there was an enormous development just around the corner. One of the friends I had made at Kill O' the Grange was David Hewlett, a brilliant young English clergyman who had been recruited by the Theological College as lecturer in systematic theology as soon as he had finished both his doctorate and his initial curacy in the Church of England. Every now and then he and his wife Penny would drop down to Dalkey for supper after the evening service or for tea before it. He would advise me on reading, respond to queries regarding theological controversies, and once or twice I attended a seminar or study day he was addressing. He was always helpful too with any problems I might have with my lecturing commitments in TCD; and it was he who was to preach in Christ Church Cathedral at the deacons' ordination service for John McCullagh, Leslie Acton, Willie Black and myself.

That summer of 1988 I was trying to get him to attend a three-day training group offered by a leading Clinical Pastoral Education supervisor from the USA at All Hallows. (This was at the request of Fr Bob Whiteside, who had placed one of his seminarians on an 'ecumenical attachment' at Kill, and had invited me to a number of pastoral training sessions at All Hallows.) In response to my pleas to David that he come along to see what went on, he came up with a proposal for me: 'Ginnie, you know they are advertising for a lecturer in applied theology at the Theological College?'

'Yes?'

'Would you consider applying for it?'

'You must be joking. I'm not even ordained yet!'

'No, but I think you'd have an awful lot to give. You've done a lot of pastoral training that is much more up-to-date and helpful than the standard fare in college, like these groups at All Hallows. I don't suppose you'd get the job, but at least they ought to hear what you have to say.'

Reckoning that I was being very cheeky, but not expecting more than the courtesy of a negative response, I did as David urged. And it was in the week of those sessions at All Hallows that I heard I was being called for interview. I think both Bob Whiteside and his co-leader in the group, Sr Moya Curran, were knocked back at the news – the thought that such a raw recruit of their own might have the chance to carry the torch to those training for ordination in the Church of Ireland.

'We'll give you every support we can, whether you get it or not,' said Bob. 'But be prepared. If you do get it, you'll also get a lot of resistance. They'll make it difficult for you until there are no students left who remember the old way of doing things.'

The interviews took place at the very end of June, just nine days after my ordination on 19 June in Christ Church Cathedral. This was a ceremony which in the event I nearly missed on account of a traffic hold-up caused by the simultaneous events of a women's mini-marathon, a vintage car rally, and the triumphant return of a football team from overseas – (a strong lesson to re-member to read the newspaper!). My arrival in the Chapter House with only minutes to spare, out of breath from racing the marathon runners along Christ Church Place, had caused some-thing of a stir; but then the archbishop caused a mild stir of his own by praying at the end of the service that I would eventually be found worthy of proceeding to the priesthood 'as far as the laws of the Church of Ireland allow'. Some people couldn't help wondering if that phrase was really in the Prayer Book!

I was similarly nearly late for the interview at the Theological College. My dear ever-obliging former rector at Kill O' the Grange had promised to have his reference as to my suitability for the position ready to be picked up at 10.15am, in good time for me to get with it to the college for the 10.55am appointment. But when I arrived at the parish office it had somehow not yet been written. And a reputation for always being late at this stage was something I could do without!

Walton Empey, the bishop in charge of Theological College matters, was fortunately in the chair and quickly put me at my ease. I don't remember the details of the interview, but Prof John Bartlett was on the panel representing TCD and Canon Hartin was present as Principal. Somehow I had found out that only two other candidates were being interviewed. One was a man from England, very well qualified but with no knowledge of the Irish scene; the other was an Irish clergyman of some seven years standing who had gone through the normal standard training at the College. He would have good pastoral experience within the Church of Ireland, but probably little familiarity with the newer methods of training for pastoral ministry. It was somewhat alarming to realise I actually had a chance of getting this job. So I answered the questions, made the best case for my-self I could, admitted that there could be difficulties with students who would resent my appointment, took my leave and left the panel to make their decision.

I headed not for home but for Co Limerick. Three years earlier, in the summer of 1985, I had been recruited by the Abbot of Glenstal, Dom Celestine Cullen, to act as co-secretary for the Glenstal Ecumenical Conference, which since starting at the ISE I had attended and enjoyed in early July every year. As a member of the committee, I was due there in time for vespers and the meal that would follow it. In a state of nervous exhaustion, I stopped for a bite of lunch in Monsterevan with Sheila Zietsman, who with one year already to her credit in the college had undertaken duty in the Church of Ireland parish there for the summer. She was intrigued to hear of the way I had spent the morning, and somewhat apprehensive at the thought of where it might lead.

Before long I was on the road again, sensing somehow that there was still an argument raging in Jim Hartin's sitting-room regarding the pros and cons of my candidacy. But the next event beckoned and soon I was thrown into the melée at the Benedictines' Normanesque castle at Murroe. The welcome was warm, and the comments on my newly donned semi-formal clerical gear reassuring, though one of the women on the committee admitted she had 'hoped you wouldn't wear the collar'. It was not the first time I had noticed that Roman Catholic women took clerical collars as symbols of hierarchical oppression, whereas I had always seen them as announcing availability and willingness to be of service.

I had barely finished explaining this when I turned round to see Walton Empey entering the foyer. I had forgotten that, as a former Bishop of Limerick, he was in the habit of attending the Glenstal Conference each year.

'Hello, Ginnie,' he greeted me. 'It's very nice to meet the new lecturer in Applied Theology at the Theological College!'

CHAPTER SEVEN

Progress at Lambeth

Can a Woman Do the Job? – The WMG Survey of women clergy

EFORE I COULD SETTLE into parish ministry, there was another Conference in the diary: in fact it was the tenth Lambeth Conference of the Bishops of the Anglican Communion, meeting in Canterbury with facilities on the campus of the University of Kent. Many women clergy and would-be clergy were planning to attend, most noticeably members of the English MOW, the American Episcopal Women's Caucus and the Australian Movement for the Ordination of Women, whose nine delegates paid their own fares to England and set up camp in the pouring rain in St Martin's camping ground.[1] I too went along at Diana McClatchey's urging, and spent time at the MOW exhibition at the Canterbury Centre and at whatever mainstream and fringe events were open to us, including a presentation by Jean Mayland to the bishops' wives. It was inspiring to us all to find a woman priest from ECUSA, the Revd Nan Peete, in the thick of the Conference as an adviser to the Bishops, and humbling to meet the Revd Florence Li Tim Oi, the Anglican Communion's first woman priest.

It was something of a surprise to find that our own Bishop John Neill was chairing the group concerned with the possibility and implications of women bishops – (the Conference had dealt with the Anglican Communion's province-by-province reception of women priests in 1978) – and that he was to lead the Conference's discussion on what seemed to us then an almost futuristic question. How did he come to be cast in such a crucial role, after a mere two years as Bishop of Tuam, the most junior

---

1. Clifford Longley, 'First impressions of Lambeth', in *The Church Times*, July 22 1988. pp 11-12.

bishopric of the Church of Ireland? In an extract from an article he wrote 1991, the bishop tells his own story:[2]

> Towards the end of 1987, I was invited to chair a small working group of the Standing Committee of the General Synod to prepare a response to certain questions relating to Ordained Ministry posed by the Seventh Meeting of the Anglican Consultative Council. I prepared draft replies to the questions surrounding the ordination of women to the priesthood and to the episcopate ... [The resultant statement] made several affirmations which still seem very important.[3]
>
> This response to the ACC was to have an immediate effect in two ways. First it hastened progress in the Church of Ireland. Second in a very personal way for me, it articulated my own hopes and ideals as I prepared to go to the Lambeth Conference ...
>
> In 1986, following the regional preparatory meetings for the Lambeth Conference, I had been assigned to the Ministry Section. I had at a later stage identified 'The Ordination of Women' as one of the subjects I would be interested in discussing further. Nevertheless, it came as a considerable surprise when a few months later I was asked to chair a group at the Conference on this topic ... Very early on, it was decided that ours would be the group that would prepare the Resolutions for the Conference on Women and the Episcopate.

---

2. John R. W. Neill, Personal Papers related to Women's Ministry Developments in the Church of Ireland.

3. These were: 1) 'A major concern of the Church of Ireland in these discussions has been to maintain a sense of unity.' 2) 'There would seem to be a growing acceptance in the Church of Ireland, not as yet put to the test, that there must be further discussion of the issue of women in the priesthood.' 3) 'It is not evident at the present time that the ordination of women to the priesthood would be the cause of schism in the province, but there are some with serious reservations about Women in the Priesthood and these would have to be respected. It is difficult to legislate for conscience without undermining authority.' 4) '... Within the Anglican Communion ... Communion does not necessarily mean full interchangeability without recognition of local authority and practice ...' 5) The Church of Ireland has ... a strong sense of its own independence within the Anglican Communion and there is a readiness to accept what is decided by bishops, clergy and laity in General Synod ... The right to be autonomous as an Episcopal Church within the Anglican Communion is only viable if it is coupled with the recognition that other provinces have the same right.'

It was in chairing long hours of these discussions that the affirmations of the previous winter took on new relevance. Whatever happened, the Resolutions presented to the Conference had to respect the autonomy of the various Provinces of the Anglican Communion, and at the same time ... that 'Communion' should not be seen as being destroyed by variety of practice with regard to women's ministry ...

The greatest problem was very naturally that those Provinces which had long ordained women felt that the Conference should be given the opportunity to affirm the ministry of these women. On the other hand [to put this to the vote] would have been extremely divisive and would possibly have caused a serious rift between Provinces. It was agreed after much thought and prayer that the unity of the Anglican Communion, the flexibility within the concept of Communion, and the independence of the individual Provinces were the matters to be affirmed by the Conference ...

In presenting the Resolutions of the Group to the Conference on 1st August 1988, I felt I was presenting something of what I had learned not only in the discussions, but within the Church of Ireland – an ability to live with difference and to accept and respect decisions properly made ...

I took from the experience of the Lambeth Conference, among many other things, three convictions which were to affect all that I did in the next eighteen months. The first was that those churches which ordained women to the priesthood could not now avoid the question of women and the episcopate. The second was that a distinction had to be made between a Province and the Anglican Communion as a whole; a province has to unambiguously affirm the ministry of all those that it ordains. The third conviction was that the ministry of women in the priesthood was a positive gift from God to the church. I had heard, I had seen and I had been persuaded.

It was with these convictions that John Neill came to his task of chairing the new Select Committee for the Ordination of Women in the Church of Ireland that autumn of 1988 – of which more later. As far as the Lambeth Conference is concerned, what should be recorded here is the resolution which he proposed in a powerful speech to the assembled bishops, and to which they gave overwhelming consent (423 in favour, 28 against, 19 abstentions):

This Conference resolves:

1. That each Province respect the decision and attitudes of other Provinces in the ordination or consecration of women to the episcopate, without such respect necessarily indicating acceptance of the principles involved, maintaining the highest possible degree of communion with the Provinces which differ.

2. That bishops exercise courtesy and maintain communications with bishops who may differ, and with any woman bishop, ensuring an open dialogue in the church to whatever extent communion is impaired.

3. That the Archbishop of Canterbury, in consultation with the Primates, appoints a commission: a) to provide for an examination of the relationships between Provinces of the Anglican Communion and ensure the process of reception includes continuing consultation with other churches as well; b) to monitor and encourage the process of consultation within the Communion and to offer further pastoral guidelines.

4. That in any Province where reconciliation on these issues is necessary, any diocesan bishop facing this problem be encouraged to seek continuing dialogue with, and make pastoral provision for, those clergy and congregations whose opinions differ from those of the bishop, in order to maintain the unity of the diocese.

5. The Conference recognises the serious hurt which would result from the questioning by some of the validity of the episcopal acts of a woman bishop, and likewise the hurt experienced by those whose conscience would be offended by the ordination of a woman to the episcopate. The church needs to exercise sensitivity, patience and pastoral care towards all concerned.[4]

The resoundingly positive vote on this five-part resolution caused much rejoicing among the women priests and their supporters around the campus and indeed around the world. It was also a strong personal affirmation for the Bishop of Tu-am (as Robert Runcie, the Archbishop of Canterbury, always announced him). If ever there was a school for mediation, it must have been the Women's Ordination Group he chaired at Lambeth. Its members had included the arch-liberal Presiding Bishop of the Episcopal Church of the USA, Edmund Browning, and the arch-conservative Bishop of London, Graham Leonard. Any one who could get those two arch-opposites to agree to a

---

4. *The Truth shall Make you Free: The Lambeth Conference 1988*, Church House Publishing 1988, p 201.

resolution, especially one concerning the ordination of women, has to have very special gifts!

* * *

FOR THREE YEARS NOW I had been part of the movement arguing that women were needed in the ordained ministry of the Church of Ireland. Now it was up to me to demonstrate the fact. If I failed, others might use my inadequacies to argue that the church had made a mistake. If I preached an indifferent sermon, if people in the back row couldn't hear me, if I appeared too attractive to the men or was less than attentive to the older women or unsympathetic to the young ones, the word would go out that 'Women can't do it!'

One of the problems, of course, was that of basic typology. One of the first to warn me of this was Harry McAdoo. His wife, Lesley, he explained, had some difficulty with the idea of women priests. 'For her, and I think for many women of her generation, the priest represents Jesus, and maybe God the Father as well; so to relate to a woman in the same way would be very difficult for her.'

The first Sunday I arrived in Bray, I encountered this very problem. A charmingly aristocratic lady of a certain age was waiting for me in the church's ample porch. 'I wanted to be the first to welcome you to the parish,' she said. 'And I also wanted to explain that while I am delighted at your arrival here as a deacon, I shan't be able to accept your ministry as a priest, if that comes about. Please don't take it personally. It's just that I am very close to the Orthodox Church and I believe as they do. But don't worry; I shan't leave the parish or anything; it's just that if you are celebrating the eucharist at some time in the future, I won't feel able to receive.'

On the other hand, my hope that many people who had doubts would come round once they saw that a woman could conduct a service in a creditable manner was fulfilled. A couple of elderly professional gentlemen, it transpired, had been sure they couldn't relate to a woman in holy orders; but they changed their minds after my first service in the parish, when as it happened the rector was away. 'Well, you've converted Charles and Albert,' I was told the next day by a former colleague of my husband's, Randall Wilson. And indeed, Charles and Albert turned out to be among my strongest supporters throughout my five years in the parish, as converts often are.

I dived into parish ministry in Bray with as little delay as possible – although a few delays there were, what with the Renewal Conference in Stranmillis immediately after my ordination and the Glenstal Conference the following week, as well as the Lambeth Conference referred to above in July.

From the day of my ordination, when my new rector David Godfrey had gathered me up at the door to the chapter house, helped me into cassock and surplice and arranged my new stole over my arm, I considered myself at his disposal for all the help I could give him in Bray parish. So at the first opportunity I set out armed with the parish list to suss out where the 'sleeping' parishioners might be found. I door-knocked my way around the outlying housing estates to introduce myself to those who had seldom been seen in church, to offer whatever help and encouragement they might need – always hoping they would come to participate in the life of the church a little more than they had before.

Only nine days into this new ministry came my unexpected recruitment to the Theological College staff. I felt apologetic to David Godfrey, almost that I had let him down; but I promised him that despite my new responsibilities I would faithfully work as many hours for the parish as would normally be expected of an auxiliary minister. And indeed it was in my interests to do so. Without a steady base in parish ministry, and as much experience in it as I could accumulate in the short time available, I knew I could not hope to supervise training in pastoral ministry for the students preparing for ordination. Fortunately I had already been undertaking hospital and nursing home visiting before ordination, as well as some house calls in Kill O' the Grange, so I was not entirely a neophyte. What was more, with no husband, no family responsibilities, and no secular job to attend to, I could make myself available more or less on a 24 hour a day basis.

Of course, my hope that I could swell the numbers in church through a concerted programme of visiting, befriending and reassuring those who had had some 'bad' experience of church in the past, were over-optimistic. Things were just not as simple as that. People were invariably welcoming – (I had considerable novelty value, after all!) – but some of their reasons for keeping their distance from the church were quite compelling. One of the parish's two churches, St Paul's at the lower end of Main Street, had been recently closed and leased out as an organ workshop. As a result, many families who could formerly walk to church in five minutes now faced a far longer uphill walk. What was worse, Christ Church, founded on land provided by the Earl of Meath in the late 19th century, was seen as the 'nobs' church' – too grand for ordinary people. Some were so angry at the closure of their church that they elected to worship elsewhere; others were so disgusted that they stopped going to any church at all. This was the beginning of my education regarding the 'non-theological factors' regarding church attendance.

Another such factor was purely architectural. Christ Church, a lofty neo-Gothic building capable of holding up to six hundred people, could have aspired to be a cathedral had it been in the right part of the diocese. It had a robed choir, an impressive organ, a remarkable reredos of saints in glittering mosaic, and stained glass windows of striking clarity and depth of colour. But its congregation was relatively small, its tradition middle-of-the-road, and it was hard under these conditions to achieve either the intimacy suitable for a small congregation or the grandeur in worship demanded by the building. However lustily and tunefully we sang, somehow one couldn't hear it. The sound 'all went up to God', as one devout and delightful lady put it.

I had to admit to myself, though to no one else, that I missed the warm, womb-like setting of my first church home at Kill O' the Grange which, being about a quarter of the size of Christ Church, with a kindly acoustic offered by the boat-shaped wooden roof, was able to offer inspirational music and spiritual intimacy at one and the same time. But now my job was to en-courage people to come to worship in this setting I would not have chosen for myself.

There was also the matter of 'churchmanship' – an anxiety factor for many newly ordained clergy as they move from their home setting to their first official position in the church.

Churchmanship for most people is concerned largely with how one behaves in church. Does one bow at the name of Jesus? Does one turn to the east for the creed? Does one embrace one's neighbours, and maybe those further afield at The Peace? Does one chant the psalms or sing versified paraphrases instead? Does one kneel, sit or stand for prayer? And for the eucharistic prayer? How often is one expected to receive communion? How long a sermon will be tolerated? Are lay people encouraged to share in leading the service?

There is a theological aspect to the 'churchmanship' issues, of course, dividing parishes roughly into 'high' (inclined to ritual, closest to Rome, and therefore rare in Ireland), broad church/ traditional (affirming traditional Christian values but allowing some liberal thinking and diversity) and 'low', which often, as well as a more evangelical emphasis on The Word, implies strong anti-Roman feelings, banning of candles, crosses, decoration and ritual 'choreography'.

The whole area of churchmanship was a key one for a number of the parish's non-attenders. The fact of the matter was that they were going elsewhere – to a church just a mile up the road which was barely part of the Church of Ireland structure, run by trustees and with its roots in the Brethren movement. It had a lot that we lacked: a smaller church, a strongly evangelical message, a degree of enthusiasm, lively music, warm fellowship, a newly built parish hall attached to the church. When those I visited admitted to going there, I did not attempt to reclaim them, having experienced for myself the importance of finding a church where the gospel 'spoke' to one. I still believe it is a matter of 'horses for courses', and my job was now to make Christian faith compelling for those who *were* willing members of the parish. Gradually, my visits came closer to the centre of the parish.

One thing that helped was the weekly prayer group, around half a dozen committed parishioners who met over coffee in the home of one or other of their number, sometimes after the Wednesday morning communion service. They were not very comfortable with the sort of spontaneous prayer I had become accustomed to, but they were faithful and warm-hearted; and as well as prayer and coffee they were generous with information about parishioners I had yet to meet, and with suggestions as to who would most welcome a visit.

I ran the gamut of old and young, male and female, sick and well, working my way through the parish list from the more to the less urgent, finding everything from kindred spirits and encouragers to one entrenched opponent. (Though polite at the time of my visit, she subsequently changed her will to direct that no woman was to minister at her funeral!) Most challenging were visits to those who were near death and had some intolerable regret or weight on their conscience. I could receive their confidences with sympathy and tell them that I was sure God would not hold past failures against them, but I could not formally pronounce God's forgiveness and grant the blessing of absolution. It became clear from personal experience that a 'permanent diaconate' for women clergy would not do.

* * *

O N THE WIDER FRONT, with three women[5] now ordained and serving in the diaconate and another, Janet Catterall, coming from England to serve in the Diocese of Cork, it was becoming clear that the Church of Ireland would soon be asked once again to make up its mind on women's ordination to the priesthood; so in the WMG we realised that simply 'keeping in touch' with conditions around the Anglican Communion was not enough. We considered carefully what needed to be done to help the process of thought and prayer required before General Synod members could see their way clear to vote.

Apart from the theological questions, there were practical considerations which were worrying those who were in principle in favour of women's priesthood. What about women's family life? How would the church structures cope with priests who needed time out for pregnancy, childbirth, child-rearing and family illnesses? Should women ordained as priests on a full-time stipendiary basis take time out or work part-time under these circumstances? Of course they should; but how would this affect their pension rights? How would parishes replace them while they were on leave or on part-time duty? Would they have

---

5. Katharine Poulton, ordained 1987, Kathleen Young and myself (both 1988)

to resign from their stipendiary position? What remuneration, if any, could they expect for their temporary part-time ministry, given that auxiliary (part-time and non-stipendiary ministers) in the Church of Ireland are paid nothing but expenses? What about women priests whose husbands also were in the ministry? Was there any reason they should not work together as a team? And if not, under what conditions?

We resolved that we would compile a questionnaire covering such issues and circulate it to women priests in the USA, Canada and New Zealand, and to women deacons or deaconesses in England, to see how they had fared in sorting out these problems. We consulted John Neill, now officially our 'link bishop', and he formally requested that we go ahead with the project and submit the results of the enquiry to the Select Committee on the Ordination of Women to the Priesthood and Episcopate which he chaired from the time of its appointment after the General Synod of 1988.

I had never compiled a questionnaire before, but with a little help from the Sociology Department in TCD, I did so.[6] We sent it off to a goodly number of women whom we contacted through their dioceses, and fielded some varied and often inspiring replies. One hundred and seven of them in all replied. I compiled a concise six-page version of the findings, directly related to our own situation, for the Select Committee on Women's Ordination, all of which, apart from the final 'Summary of Suggestions', found its way into the General Synod Reports for 1990, the year of the final vote. The suggestions are still of interest however, since they pose questions which remain relevant to the conditions of ministry for women clergy and their families – questions relating to child-rearing, time out, pension rights and shared ministry being among the most important.[7]

However by the autumn 1989 doing justice to the wealth of accounts of women's experience was beyond my resources of time and space, so we asked Margaret Larminie (formerly education officer of the Church of Ireland) to undertake the task for us, with a view to making the results available to the Anglican Consultative Council (ACC), the body of lay and ordained

6. See Appendix 1 for the full Questionnaire.
7. See Appendix II.

members of all the Anglican Provinces which as early as 1971 had given an important lead to the introduction of women's ordained ministry as each church saw fit to introduce it.[8] The 37-page document she produced is available in the Representative Church Body Library in Dublin under the title *Conditions and Deployment of Married Women Clergy in the Anglican Communion*.

* * *

LOOKING BACK on my first year and a half of parish ministry, it is clear that it would have been a full one even without my 'full-time' job at the Theological College, which will be the subject of the next chapter. One of the most meaningful things I did in the parish did not begin until a little after I was priested, which is to anticipate; but I hope readers will forgive me for giving an account of it here.

This was an enquiry and exploration group called The Monday Club, which I started in response to spontaneous demands for something of the kind from three different women. After announcing in church one day that I was offering to host a 'no questions barred' group in the Parish Life Centre (the pre-fab behind the church) the following Monday evening, I was almost surprised to find that six women duly turned up. I asked them to suggest areas they would like to explore, or simply to share 'where they were at'. My brief notes from the session read as follows:

- Difficulty of faith, when love and hope seem absent.
- Difficulty of prayer without group support (especially the new Healer Prayer arrangement, where group members are asked to pray daily at home)
- Difficulty in making own decisions in face of family pressures.
- Guilt.

---

8. Acting on a request from the Lambeth Conference of 1968, the meeting of the Anglican Consultative Council in Limuru, Kenya, in 1971, declared in Resolution 28 b) that 'This Council advises the Bishop of Hong Kong, acting with the approval of his Synod, and any other Bishop of the Anglican Communion acting with approval of his Province, that if he decides to ordain women to the priesthood, his action will be acceptable to this Council, and that this Council will use its good offices to encourage all Provinces of the Anglican Communion to continue in communion with these dioceses.'

- Baptism with water *and the Holy Spirit*?
- The relationship of Eastern religions to Christianity.
- How to pray!
- One person said she was a non-believer; one said she was an agnostic; all wanted to 'listen and learn'.

Then a note of questions suggested during the following week:

- Is belief necessary?
- What is God's attitude to unbelievers?

As the reader can imagine, we had lots of work ahead of us. So much, indeed, that although the membership fluctuated over the next three years of three Monday evening sessions each month, there was always reluctance to stop for the summer holidays. I look back on that group as the most stimulating, and stimulated, I ever worked with, although I had a lot to learn about maintaining boundaries with those ultra-needy of my attention.

In addition to this group, and many more ups and downs of parish life which could be recorded, two meaningful experiences of personal ministry stand out as I look back.

My cousin Penny Gundry, who had first come to Dublin at my invitation while still a student at York University, had met the man she was to marry at Kill O' the Grange. An October 1988 wedding was planned and the couple invited me to conduct the ceremony, which was to be followed by a reception in the newly opened parish hall. The big question: could a deacon legally officiate at a wedding in the Church of Ireland? There was no doubt that it had been done, but considerable doubt as to whether it was legal. I fought hard for permission to do the deed, but expert opinion advised against it, although I was permitted to assist. Through nervousness, I gave the dismissal twice, once before and once after the final hymn – but the bridegroom kindly said this made the ceremony all the better!

The other special event was a particularly sad one. My best friend and neighbour from the early seventies, fellow Englishwoman Jane Gebler, was found by her husband Ernie collapsed in the front garden, moaning 'Help me.' A few days later she died in Beaumont Hospital, without ever having regained consciousness, still only around 50 years old. Ernie was at a loss as to funeral arrangements and, as we stood forlornly in a corridor in the hospital, asked me what would be the proper thing to do, even assenting, in a stunned way, to a prayer at her bedside. Simultaneously the Church of Ireland chaplain at Beaumont asked the rector of Dalkey if he knew Jane, or failing that, whether he knew of any pastoral support for the family. 'Funnily enough, it's Ginnie,' he replied, only weeks after I had been ordained. And the strange fact was that not long before, Jane had asked me to take her to the early service in Dalkey, for reasons that I sensed to be not entirely spiritual – (for both she and Ernie had for years been principled non-believers).

However, we opted not to have the funeral service in Dalkey. Instead, I conducted the simplest possible service at the crematorium in Glasnevin. A couple of young relations of Jane's came over from England to say goodbye, but otherwise my recollection is that the service was attended only by Ernie and the staff and students from Sandford Park, where Jane had been the highly valued Headmistress of the Junior School for many years. It was the first funeral I had ever conducted and one of the most difficult and most moving, committing the soul of a dear, generous and often anxious friend into the arms of the Creator and Redeemer she had never been able to acknowledge. Somehow, despite all the 'conditions' regarding belief of the funeral liturgy, I had confidence that she would receive a loving welcome from the One who knows the secrets of all hearts.

CHAPTER EIGHT

The General Synod of 1989

Early days at the College; the Big Debate; 'Concerned Clergy'

C ANON JIM HARTIN, the Principal of the Theological College, had been in favour of the ordination of women for many years and had been good enough to address a WMG group in Trinity College on one occasion. He had supervised the three year training period of our first woman ordinand, Katharine Poulton, the first of a trickle of women ordinands which would grow to a flood after the way to priesthood opened for them in 1990; and he had shown his confidence in women's abilities also by employing Bet Aalen, an Old Testament specialist associated with TCD, to teach Biblical Studies in the Professional Diploma in Theology, which at that time was the approved route to ordained ministry.

Nonetheless, he seemed somewhat nervous about my appointment, and so did my friend Sheila Zietsman, now coming into her second year at the college, sensing that it would be difficult to remain friends with me while also retaining her place as 'one of the boys' in the college. Obviously there was going to be resistance from the student body to being taught the practical and pastoral side of their calling by a woman who had little track record in the field herself, and who had not even submitted, as they had to, to the three-year 'internment' that was required of all future stipendiary clergy.

Jim was welcoming to me and declared himself 'delighted to have you with us on the staff', but he monitored my words, deeds, schedules and body language carefully, and within the first six weeks placed in my pigeon-hole two six page handwritten epistles of fatherly guidance and administrative caution. For example:

> You will need to slip obliquely into the work. The temptation is to rush in with vigour and sound, but this is unwise. Give people

time to get used to your presence – they will be watching your every step and weighing every word, and assessing you by word and action. It is never wise to act or speak without *considerable* reflection – mistakes are not soon forgotten in a place like our college. You will need to win support *gradually*. You will be particularly watched because you sound 'English'. This is still a threat to simple Irish people! I never want to hear any one say, 'She doesn't understand; she's not one of us …'

Jim continued in this vein, warning especially of the dangers of overwork and insufficient time to relax in solitude, and emphasising also the students' need for privacy and the importance of paying no attention to their gossip. He concluded:

P.S. Please just make sure of clearing any new things with me – I have in the end to carry all we do with the House of Bishops and they expect that I will take responsibility for all any member of staff does! I love to do fresh things, but I need to know in advance.

I was indeed 'doing fresh things' – and with Jim Hartin's approval. It had been found that the previous system of integrating pastoral and practical experience with the academic study programme provided too much distraction from the required reading and essay-writing, so I had been asked to arrange three weeks of full-time pastoral and practical experience and reflection to precede the academic work scheduled for mid-October. From a standing start on 1 September, this was quite a tall order, so the principal's caution to avoid overwork and high levels of stress in the planning period was understandable enough. All the same, his contention that 'we have plenty of time – all the time God gives us' seemed to me more pious hope than fact!

Looking at the old schedules at the back of my filing cabinet today, I find it surprising that I managed in the time available to get such a programme together – three weeks of different daily programmes for both the second and third year students, plus one introductory week for the first years. But with the help of friends and contacts made over the years, in Church of Ireland parishes, at All Hallows, in TCD, through journalism, on the AA network and, added to those, some brass-necked requests to complete strangers over the telephone, it was done. And on the whole the students reacted well and were appreciative.

One of the 'fresh things', though, was less than popular with them – the dreaded *verbatim*. The presentation by tyro pastors of verbatim reports of their contacts with those they are trying to help was by then a standard training tool in seminaries and pastoral institutes worldwide – one that I had encountered and benefited from both at the Westminster Pastoral Foundation and at All Hallows; but it was still unknown in the college. Having learned so much from the process myself, I had little doubt that this simple method of pastoral reflection could only be beneficial all round. It involved recalling exactly what had been said in an interview, along with the facial expressions, body language, pauses and tone of voice, and then reflecting with the help of one's peers and the group's leader on what had been going on, what traps might have been sprung, what revelations made on either side, and how best to improve the pastoral relationship. The method can be expanded to include deep theological, sociological and psychological observations, but we kept it simple:

> What was your understanding of the person and your aim?
> What did each of you say and do?
> What effect did this have?
> Is there anything you would wish to change on a 're-play'?
> How do you see the future of this interaction?

It was a method of learning from experience which I had found invaluable, but the students hated it. I even had to receive a deputation of objectors from the third year, who felt that their precious 'privacy' was being invaded, when they ambushed me on the wide granite staircase leading from the dining-hall to the principal's apartment. I suppose I had reckoned without two things: the overcrowded 'fish bowl' social structure of the college community which made vulnerability of any kind unacceptable, and the secretive instincts developed in the interest of self-preservation over generations in the North, where careless spills of information could cost even one's life.

Nonetheless I continued to insist on the students taking turns at presenting verbatims. On one occasion I received one which was purely fictitious; but Bob Whiteside reassured me: 'You can tell as much from a made-up verbatim as from a real one. Look for the words that come up most often. Look for the attitudes just beneath the surface. A student can learn as much about him or herself from an incident they have invented as from one that really happened – sometimes more.' I recalled that he had warned me I would encounter resistance to anything new, until there was no one left who remembered the old way of doing things. And my response to resistance, rightly or wrongly, was to persevere.

The resistance, though, was more hurtful than I admitted to myself at the time. I had gone into the job imagining that I could demonstrate to the students that we were all 'on the same side'; that I understood well where they were coming from, the problems they had to contend with, and wanted to be their ally in overcoming them. Such hopes were naïve, of course; and before long I had to accept that in certain contexts I was seen as 'the enemy'.

* * *

ONLY SEVEN MONTHS after my first academic year opened at the Theological College, the Church of Ireland was facing into the General Synod of 1989. The Synod of 1988 had appointed a new Select Committee 'to consider the theological, practical and other implications of the ordination of women priests to the service of the Church of Ireland and the liturgical changes and legal procedures required...' The Committee, chaired by Bishop John Neill, was to report to the 1989 General Synod, meeting on 16-18 May in the Royal Dublin Society in Ballsbridge, Dublin 4.

Its report was generally considered to be comprehensive, both theologically and practically; it was also measured and objective, detailing the pros and cons in a manner deemed fair by both sides of the debate. The most controversial question, perhaps, lay towards the end of the report in a passage justifying the decision of the 1988 Synod that, when it came to a vote on women's priesthood, the Synod should vote simultaneously on their acceptability as bishops. Many of us in the WMG feared that this could lose the vote for women; but Michael Kennedy who had seconded Dean John Paterson's proposal to 'include women bishops' argued, as did the Select Committee, that if women priests were barred from the episcopate theirs would be a 'second-class' priesthood.

If this anxiety did not offer *frisson* enough for the fervent supporters of women's ordination, the resolution appended to the report certainly did. It asked for 'leave to be granted for the introduction of a Bill in the General Synod of 1990 to enable women to be ordained as priests and bishops, and to make consequential changes to the formularies of the church.'[1]

It was just as well that term at the Theological College was nearly over at this stage, with the students heavily involved in exams. Though of course not a member of Synod (this being at that stage impossible for women clergy, all of whom had been ordained deacon since the last elections to the General Synod) I was able to go and sit with former colleagues on the press benches, to watch, listen and take note of all that was going on.

The debate was beautifully managed both by Archbishop Eames, who chaired the proceedings, and by John Neill, who introduced the debate. He began by reminding the Synod of the basic question to be answered: 'To put it bluntly, the question is whether the church which is faithful to the gospel should have women priests and women bishops, or whether such a development is contrary to the same gospel.' In support of a positive vote he offered three thoughts: 1. Recent developments in theology and biblical studies had emphasised that humanity embraced both male and female, while both male and female imagery was used of God. 2. The Anglican Communion at this point already had at least twelve hundred women priests, and the experience of their ministry had been positive. 3. Those anxious about ecumenical counter-indications should note that although the attitude of the Roman Catholic hierarchy was negative, 'yet we also hear in many parts of the world among members of that church a growing demand for women priests'. He concluded: 'Could it be that God who sent forth his Son born of a woman might once more use womankind to present his Son to a sadly broken world?'

Three hours of debate followed, which often had us on the edge of our seats as we inwardly cheered or booed the speakers, although there was really nothing new being said, apart from an occasional memorable phrase. I still remember Archbishop Donald

---

1. 1989 Select Committee Report, p 247.

Caird suggesting that a precipitate vote in favour of such a momentous departure from tradition would liken the assembly to a herd of lemmings, hurling themselves from a cliff-top in a leap of suicidal proportions. And many others expressed their anxieties about the timing in less striking terms.

But Bishop Neill, aware that it was most of all the voice of caution that might sway the Synod against the motion, urged in his summing-up that the vote at this time was still not decisive, and that the Synod could, if it wished, postpone a final decision on the matter for two years instead of one, in which case he would not reintroduce the matter until 1991. For now, this was a vote in principle. (And indeed, it might have been pointed out, the same had been said of the Synod's positive vote 13 years ago, in 1976!) His concession carried the day, and it was hard to restrain our delight (as pictures in the next day's papers witnessed) when the result was announced: 73% of the clergy in favour, and a whopping 87% of the laity. The two-thirds clerical vote required to carry the motion was passed with room to spare.

Sitting there near the front of the hall in my black shirt and clerical collar, I was an obvious target for the photographers and the microphones. 'Don't be too triumphant,' Archdeacon Gordon Linney hissed at me as I passed him. 'Tell them, it's just part of a process!' 'It's just part of a process,' I echoed as the mikes invaded my space. 'Of course I'm very pleased at the result; but there's still a long way to go.'

And indeed there was; but not as far as it might have seemed at the time.

The major challenge, later that year, came from 'The Concerned Clergy' a disparate group of clerical objectors, a mix of high churchmen worried about relations with Rome and conservative evangelicals who considered any 'headship' of women to be contrary to biblical teaching. Dean John Paterson of Christ Church Cathedral, Dublin, Canon John Crawford of St Patrick's Cathedral, Canon Victor Stacey, Rector of Santry, Peter Barrett, chaplain of TCD, and Willy Bridcut, superintendent of Irish Church Missions, had met in Dublin late in June, five weeks after the close of the Synod, to discuss what could be done. With the support of five more 'concerned' colleagues, Ken Clarke, then rector of Coleraine, John McCarthy, Dean of Clogher,

Robert Townley, Dean of Ross, Henry Gilmore, rector of Achill and Christopher Wilcock of Stoneyford in Connor Diocese, they issued a 'Questionnaire' to all clergy of the Church of Ireland, which aimed to field figures to persuade the Synod that a considerable proportion of serving clergy had serious doubts about the priesthood of women, and that the legal movement in this direction had been 'unduly hasty'.

The questionnaire angered any one who seriously supported the motion before the Synod, chiefly because the three questions which followed the factual ones regarding the acceptability of women priests and bishops were so 'loaded' towards a No vote:

Do you approve of the Church of Ireland moving in this matter with what, to some, seems undue haste?

If, in November 1989, the Church of England decides against ordaining women, would you still approve of the Church of Ireland going it alone?

Should account be taken of its effect on relations with other churches?

And, although the tenor of the letter introducing the questionnaire on the surface made some pretence of open-mindedness, for example, 'We would not claim the ordination of a woman to be an impossibility but we do believe that, for whatever reason, the matter is being implemented with undue haste', it was clear that this was an attempt to scupper the Bill to be introduced in 1990 or 1991. The letter's final sentence, 'Our aim is to maintain the unity, catholicity and apostolicity of the church we love and serve,' underlined this.

The letter and attached questionnaire were sent to every bishop, priest and deacon in the Church of Ireland, whether retired, stipendiary or auxiliary, with the request to reply by 30 September. About two thirds of the clergy replied; but not all responded to the questions, many respondents declaring that they were unanswerable as put. My own rector, David Godfrey wrote:

Dear Brothers,

I was annoyed and then disappointed by your letter and questionnaire. As I read it more closely I felt insulted by some of the implications. I understood the trap that 'concern' sets for all who have deep convictions and so I am hoping that friendship and fellowship will not be impaired by either my response or the effect on others of this unfortunate communication.

The problem of 'undue haste' reminds me of my mother's re-action when Heather and I decided to get married after six years' preparation. 'What is all the rush about?' was the cry. Talk about undue haste is very similar in this case, considering the years that this matter has been on the agenda of General Synod.

Furthermore, I am saddened that the letter and the question-naire should be cast in such loaded terms which place all who com-plete the latter in a 'Catch 22' situation and reduces such an import-ant matter to music hall proportions. In question 3, one is faced with a similar catch to the old trick question as to whether one has stopped beating the wife yet.

This response may seem almost frivolous but I assure you that nothing could be further from the truth. If the opportunity to fur-ther the discussion in a spirit of understanding and openness, where all could speak frankly and seek together for an answer founded on the gospel, I would do all I could to foster it and encour-age others to participate.

Yours sincerely,

David Godfrey, Christ Church, Bray, September 15th 1989

It was gratifying to find, when David shared this letter with me later on, that he felt so strongly. Before mentioning the Concerned Clergy communication to him I discussed it with friends in the Women's Ministry Group, especially with Daphne Wormell. While we were appalled at what seemed to us a shameless attempt to alter the mind of General Synod through soliciting and publicising the answers they wanted through a loaded questionnaire, we were disinclined to reply in kind. (Our own more complex, scientific and objective questionnaire, re-ferred to in the last chapter, was at this stage already in train.) Instead, we felt that we as the WMG needed to contrive to meet these 'concerned clergy' as a group, to attempt to understand their feelings but also to ask that they appreciate ours, so that even while we disagreed there could be some sense of mutual compassion between us. It was at this point that we resolved to invite them to a type of *colloquium*, which took place in the Salle d'Armes – (no significance in the location intended!) – in Sandymount that winter. But we also felt that their letter and questionnaire needed to be challenged, and this I undertook to do personally, since to compose a letter to be adjusted, voted on and signed by the membership of the Women's Ministry Group would just take too long. This is what I wrote:

Dear Brothers in Christ,

How glad I am that in Christ there is no male or female. Otherwise your communication might tempt me to despair. It is nonetheless very disappointing that you should see fit to attempt this sort of pressure in a matter which is at present before the General Synod, as indeed it has been on a regular basis for the last thirteen years at the very least.

Until now I was happy that we in the Church of Ireland had managed to avoid any polarisation on this issue, and it seemed that we were all content to be guided gradually by the Holy Spirit to move forward according to God's will at the pace appropriate for our church. Your action seems to me to threaten all that. Yet I hope it is still not too late for people of differing views on the matter to meet to listen to each other and attempt to understand each other's position in a spirit of Christian love. I think I have already suggested to some of you – those whose position I knew – that I would welcome such a conversation, either individually or in a mixed group.

As I hope you will understand, I am not in a position to complete your questionnaire because the last three questions are so 'loaded' as to be unanswerable. My belief is that the churches of the Anglican Communion should move on this matter, under God, at the pace right for their own people, not looking over their shoulders to see how sister churches or other denominations are proceeding. I also understand this view to be in line with the recommendations of both the Lambeth Conference and the Anglican Consultative Council.

I do hope that you will reconsider the approach you are currently taking on this matter. I do not believe that it will be of any advantage either to you personally or to the Church of Ireland, or indeed to our Communion, as a whole.

I hope also that you can accept me, as you address me, as truly you sister in Christ, who shares your humanity and his.

Sincerely,

Ginnie Kennerley, September 17th 1989

Of course the trouble with this type of written communication is always that while each letter seems eminently reasonable to its writer, the recipients read it through their own particular lenses. It was reported to me by a mutual colleague that Victor Stacey said he 'choked on his cornflakes' when confronted with my letter in his morning post. Nonetheless, it was to his credit that he wrote me by return of post a very civil reply the first half of which ran as follows:

> Dear Ginnie,
> Your communication received this morning warrants a brief reply. I am sorry you are taking the contents of the letter so personally because such was not my intention, nor as I understand it the intention of the other signatories. What we hope to encourage is exactly what you are suggesting – greater debate and more open discussion – so that at the end of the day the vote may be in accordance with the best traditions of Anglicanism, scripture, tradition, reason, conscience, under the guidance of the Holy Spirit. God forbid that any should regard it as an occasion for scoring points.

He went on to discuss our work together with students at the Theological College, where I had enlisted his help as one of a group of 'pastoral supervisors' for some of the students, offering to resign if I now felt uncomfortable having him on the team. I felt that his letter boded well for some degree at least of civility, courtesy and consideration between those of different views in this area, and so it has proved to be.

The meeting at the Salle D'Armes took place on 29 January 1990, and as I recall a sincere attempt was made on both sides to respect the feelings of those committed to the opposite position. In fact the 'Concerned Clergy' group invited us to attend the Pre General Synod Conferences that they were planning for 3 and 4 May, in Belfast and Dublin respectively. Without exception, I think we all attempted to demonstrate Christian courtesy and forbearance; but convictions were by now too firmly held on either side for any deeply sympathetic listening or indeed conversions to be possible. It did, however, demonstrate that the supporters of women's ministry were no 'monstrous regiment of women' but reasonable and courteous individuals who desired not to cause pain but to promote harmony and healing. And our male opponents were as courteous as we could have hoped in a setting which must have been difficult enough for them.

* * *

At the 1976 General Synod:
Above: Archbishop Alan Buchanan *(photo Tom Lawlor, © Irish Times)*
Right: Catherine McGuinness

An early mentor: The Revd Cecil Kerr of the Christian Renewal Centre, Rostrevor. *(photo © Beryl Stone)*

Know Your Faith tapes meeting in 1983. *Left to right:* Liz Orr, Revd Ricky Rountree, Revd Ken Clarke, the author, Rend Coslett Quin and Revd Billy Gibbons.

Two early encouragers: *Left:* Revd Stanley Baird, *Right:* Archbishop Harry McAdoo

Participants at the WMG Conference 1986

Above left: Dss Diana McClatchey, *Right*: Daphne Wormell
Below left: Archbishop John Armstrong, *Right*: Bishop Samuel Poyntz

Steps on the way:
Above: The author with Professor Seán Freyne in TCD Graduation Day 1986.
Below: With Revd Billy Gibbons and Archbishop Donald Caird after commissioning as a Lay Reader, 1.11.86

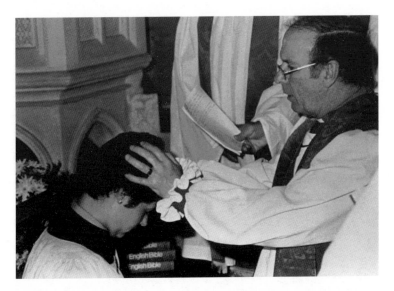

Above: The first woman deacon, Revd Katharine Poulton, ordained by Bishop Gordon McMullan. *photo:©Pacemaker*

Below left: Revd Katharine Poulton, *photo:©Pacemaker.*

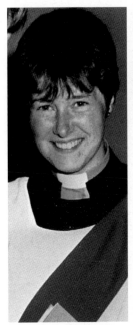

Above: First Dublin ordinations to the diaconate. The author with Revd Dr David Hewlett (preacher) and Revd John McCullagh, 19.5.1988.

Lambeth 1988 Above: Bishop John Neill addresses the Conference. *photo Matt Kavanagh ©Irish Times.*
Below: Women priests of historic significance. *Left*: Revd Florence Li Tim Oi of Hong Kong, *Right*: Revd Nan Peete of ECUSA, adviser to the Lambeth Conference

At the General Synod 1990. *Above:* Archbishop Robin Eames. *photo Phil Carrick © Irish Times.*

Below Left: Canon Jim Hartin, *Right:* Dean John Paterson.

1990: The first ordinations. *Above:* Revd Kathleen Young and Revd Irene Templeton.
Below: Revd Janet Catterall with Bishop Roy Warke and Dean Maurice Carey. *photo © Irish Examiner*

Above: The author as Harvest preacher at the Church of The Holy Redeemer in Bray with Revd Fr John O'Connell PP, Rev Stuart Morris (Methodist), Revd David Godfrey, rector of Bray, 18.9.1992.
Below: Declaration at Castledermot institution with registrar Walter Fisher, church wardens and Archbishop Donald Caird, 23.10.1990. *photo©Bray Photo Lab*

Above: Castledermot institution: After the ceremony with Ven Cecil Price, Revd David Godfrey, Prof John Bartlett and Archbishop Caird, 23.10.1990. *Photo©Thomas Sunderland*
Below: Raising church roof funds with Archbishop Caird, 13.5.1994. *Photo©Bray Photo Lab*

Above: At the Timolin NS opening in November 1996, Archbishop Walton Empey, Alan Dukes TD, the author, Carol Glynn, Cllr Rainsford Hendy.
Right: With Archbishop Empey at my installation as a Canon of Christ Church Cathedral, January 1997.

Above: With Revd Anne Taylor and Revd Susan Green preparing for the service to celebrate ten years of women priests, 3.9.2000.

Below: With Dean Paterson and the first women lay readers of Dublin and Glendalough Diocese: Daphne Wormell, Patricia Hastings-Hardy, Audrey Smith and Thea Boyle, after preaching at their twenty-fifth anniversary service in Christ Church Cathedral, 19.12.2000.

THE UNCERTAINTY about the position and responsibilities of women clergy in the Church of Ireland was difficult all round, not least because until D-Day opinion could still be swayed in either direction. Both the WMG and the Concerned Clergy continued to do what they could to encourage the 'right' decision to be made.

WMG meetings and social events continued, with our annual Quiet Day in December 1989 being conducted by Bishop Brian Hannon of Clogher; but most of our effort for the rest of the year went into the Anglican Communion Women's Ministry Research Project. As mentioned earlier, we also hosted two women from the other side of the Atlantic and had some helpful conversations with them, the Revd Noreen Mooney, who was in charge of a small parish in Long Island, though still a deacon, and the Revd Alice Medcof, who we had already met the preceding year at Lambeth. Alice was a high-powered Canadian rector, who was tipped as a future bishop at the time.

There was a sense at this point that argumentation was no longer the most important thing. The people who were going to be swayed by biblical exposition and objective reasoning had already taken up their positions. Many of those still hesitating, we felt, were probably doing so more for emotional reasons, possibly connected with women's place in the home, which was being addressed by our research project. Others no doubt were sincerely pondering what was the will of God on the question. With these in mind, and indeed for all of us, I wrote these *Prayers for 1990*, which we both used at WMG meetings and offered to the church at large:

Eternal God
who created us male and female in your image
and made us all one in Christ Jesus,
renew us by your Spirit
that as women and men together
we may build your church
and serve your people,
in Jesus' name. Amen.

God of love and truth
you teach us that we cannot love you
unless we love our sisters and brothers

and you promise that the truth will set us free;
open all eyes to your truth
and all hearts to your love
to lead your church in harmony to the ministry you desire
that your good news may come to all people. Amen.

Heavenly Father
whose love casts out all fear,
so perfect your church in love
that we may know no fear
but follow bravely where your Spirit leads
united in Christ our Lord. Amen.

There was one other anxiety, apparently superficial, yet powerful if left unchallenged – simply some traditionally-minded people's perception of the way women should or should not present themselves in terms of their general deportment and apparel.

In my early days at the Theological College, I was very struck by the vehemence with which the Revd Noel Shortt, then serving in the Diocese of Derry, deplored the appearance of a woman cleric wearing a trouser suit! 'Trying to look like a man' seemed to be the problem, the idea being that women trying to be priests were women denying their own femininity. I've no idea how representative his views were, but they influenced me greatly. For all my time at the college, I don't think I ever appeared in trousers, although I always wore a clerical collar as a matter of principle and favoured fairly sober colours and a sort of 'smart casual' look, which I was later told influenced some of our women ordinands when their time came.

The clerical collar was a problem for some. I think it was the rector of Altar in Cork Diocese, who remarked over dinner in the college one evening, that he didn't think clerical collars suited women. 'They don't look too great on some men!' I couldn't help retorting; and frankly I still think the 'dog collar' looks very smart on women.

Older women had similar difficulties. I well remember going to preach at King's Hospital on Pentecost Sunday in 1989. As usual, I prepared the sermon carefully for the congregation concerned and also dressed with care – a collarless black linen jacket, a beige and black check cotton skirt, a black clerical shirt with

'Roman' collar, black court shoes and suntan coloured tights. For the chaplain Revd Matthew Byrne's wife at least, it was the sartorial care, not the homiletic skill, which was the winner. 'You look so elegant and yet so dignified,' she said – or words to that effect. 'I was dreading what you'd look like, but it's absolutely right!'

On such apparently insignificant details, I imagine, a number of votes changed from 'No' to 'Aye' the following year may have depended.

CHAPTER NINE

1990: 'All Three Houses vote Aye'

The first women priests; Synod 1991: is recognising women priests optional?

D ESPITE ALL the pre-Synod anxiety, many Church of Ireland people had expected no clear-cut decision at the General Synod of 1990. This was because Bishop Neill, when summing up at the 1989 Synod, had undertaken to propose in 1990 that the final debate and vote on the Bill providing for the ordination of women as priests and bishops be postponed until 1991 'in order to enable further consideration of its implications'. The idea behind this, as witnessed by a 1989 General Synod memo, was to allow a 'cooling off period', though it may equally have been a tactical concession to secure the votes of those worried about 'undue haste'.

However, those in the know became aware early in 1990 that there was a move afoot for the promised amendment to be 'not put'. John Neill himself adverted to this in April1990 in an article in the *Church of Ireland Gazette*, which prompted me to write to him some ten days before the Synod urging caution. I wrote in part:

> More and more over the past few weeks I have been hearing people, especially clergy who are hesitating about how to vote, saying that they do not want to be hurried or pressurised into a vote which they consider premature, and that the effect of this will be to make them vote 'No'. This applies to clergy from both catholic and evangelical wings of the church, North and South. I have told anyone who mentioned the matter to me personally that I assume the Synod will have the chance to vote formally on whether or not they will agree to the amendment being withdrawn, and that this in itself is as good as voting on the amendment itself, but most people seem to assume the opposite ...
>
> As far as the Women's Ministry Group is concerned, I believe I speak for us all in saying that much though we would like to see the measure go through in 1990, we would hate to see it long-fingered

for the best part of a decade through a perceived 'rushing of the fences' this year.

When the bishop rose at the 1990 Synod to say in effect that he was now asking the Synod to allow him to withdraw his promised amendment, so that the Bill could be debated and voted on at the current Synod, there was audible reaction from the floor of the House. Indeed there were some who felt they had been deceived, although the Synod did indeed vote to approve the withdrawal of the amendment without serious difficulty. It was more of a hiccup than a stumbling block in the process, but the protests rumbled on in Letters to the Editor and letters to the bishop for some months to come. So what was the explanation for this marked change of tactics?

A portion of a personal letter to Bishop Neill[1] from one of the lay honorary secretaries of the General Synod, Barry Deane of Cork Diocese, dated 23 May 1989, goes some way to explaining the *volte-face*:

> I feel strongly that the legislation should be enacted next year, and that you should not proceed with your 1991 amendment. My reasons are:
> 1. 1990 is an election year for the House of Representatives, and a final decision in 1991 opens the door to canvassing.
> 2. Uncertainty would be re-created because of the influx of new members into the Synod in 1991.
> 3. The Synod will be expecting a further vote by division. It is almost impossible to hold one without causing chaos in Belfast City Hall; all of the doors are on the chairman's left, and they lead onto a corridor; if you turn right, you are some distance from the nearest open area, and if you turn left you are in a cul-de-sac.

None of these reasons was given by Bishop Neill when he rose to speak. Instead he argued strongly that the church was now ready to make this decision, and that to delay further would adversely affect its morale and its witness. Proposing the Bill itself, he gave a strong speech, centred on the theme 'The time is now', which did not attempt to summarise the arguments in favour – these by now being so well known.

---

1. The letter was kindly provided by Archbishop Neill along with other papers relating to the debate on women's ordination.

The way had been most ably prepared for him by the Primate, Most Revd Robin Eames, in his presidential address opening the Synod. Referring to the issue, he said it was 'undoubtedly the item of business before the Synod this week which will attract most interest within and without the church'. He continued: 'I do not believe it to be my duty ... to seek to influence the Synod in matters which must be for the individual conscience of each member.' But he wanted to draw attention to four points in particular. First, the church had had 'the opportunity to discuss the question over an extensive period' – ten years had gone by since permission had first been sought to introduce a Bill allowing the ordination of women as priests. Second, whichever way the Synod voted, it would have repercussions on the Church of Ireland's relationship with the other churches of the Anglican Communion. Third, whatever decision was reached, there would be a minority left less than happy by the decision. 'That minority deserves the full consideration, respect and understanding of the majority,' he stressed, 'They have a perfect right to their views and the last thing I want to see in the Church of Ireland is any sense of victory or defeat.' He pledged that he would do all in his power to take measures to ensure that all members of the church could continue to relate to one another with compassion and mutual understanding. Finally, he appealed for all to approach the proceedings prayerfully and in a spirit of openness to God's will for the church.

The debate itself was considerably less exciting than the previous year; but the stress was extreme. We well knew that around ten clerical votes could decide the matter one way or the other. We knew also that there had been a move, initiated by the Dean of Christ Church, John Paterson, to block the Bill on the grounds that such legislation could be legally challenged on the grounds that the Preamble to the Constitution laid down at Disestablishment in 1870 that the orders of bishops, priests and deacons would be kept 'inviolate' by the church. The fact that the Legal Advisory Committee had ruled against such an interpretation[2] did not entirely guarantee that the matter would not be raised again in debate to encourage opposition.

2. The LAC responded to a query from the Select Committee on the Ordination of Women to the effect that the phrase in the Preamble had

What Dean Paterson did in the debate in fact introduced a new element – a strong request for a 'conscience clause' to protect clergy who could not in conscience accept the priestly ministry of women. The suggestion was set aside by Bishop Neill in summing up the debate, on the grounds that the Church of Ireland was a caring church which would ensure that the views and the status of the minority would be respected. However, the demand was to return with renewed strength the following year, threatening to make the priesthood of women a kind of optional extra in the church's ministry, which might at some time be discontinued. More of that later.

The vote on the second reading of the Bill, taken on the first day of the Synod, Tuesday 15 May, brought a sigh of relief and delight to its many supporters, especially the WMG observers seated in the back rows reserved for visitors; and on the press benches it was hard to conceal my feelings. I remember turning to Patrick Comerford, who was covering for the *Irish Times*, with a quiet cat-got-the-cream smile. The voting was as follows: House of Clergy: in favour, 129; against, 59 (69% to 31%); House of Laity: in favour 232; against, 29 (a massive 89% to 11%). This was handsomely over the two-thirds majority required in both houses; and yet we could still not relax. The third reading of the Bill still had to pass on the Thursday, and it would take only the change of three or four clerical votes for the Bill to fail.

Deaconess Diana McClatchey, who had come over from her home in Worcestershire to support us, could bear it no longer. She headed back home on the Wednesday evening boat, promising that her prayers for us would be unceasing.

Next day, we scanned the assembly anxiously, fearful that too many of the 'Aye' voters might have gone home early (as far-flung members of Synod have often been inclined to do) and that the Bill would fall at the last fence. But we need not have worried. The percentages on the final vote confirmed a slight improvement in the clerical vote (69.6% as against 69%) al-

---

referred not to who might serve in holy orders, but to the danger at that time of a 'presbyterianisation' of Anglican orders, which would have seen the episcopate being reduced to the status merely of senior priests of the church.

though the total number voting was very slightly less, and a slightly decreased percentage in favour from the laity – 86%, which was still 20% more than the percentage required for the Bill to pass.[3] Still the House of Bishops had to vote, for which purpose they adjourned to a private room. They returned to announce that their votes showed 'a majority' in favour. They declined to specify the numbers for and against, but it was generally believed to have been 9-3. We knew, of course, that the Archbishop of Dublin, Donald Caird, must have been one of the 'No' voters; but to his great credit he accepted the vote without rancour or further comment as the decision of the Church of Ireland.

That very afternoon, work at the Theological College being in abeyance, I took off from Dublin Airport to visit my ailing stepmother to the west of Birmingham. I was glad to be out of the reach of the press and away from the possibility of meeting disconsolate 'No' voters around Dublin or Bray. The train from Birmingham Airport to Stourbridge in those days required a change at Birmingham Central. Imagine my astonishment when I got into the train there to find myself in the same carriage as Diana McClatchey. 'Diana! We're through!', I greeted her. And indeed she had not heard the good news, having been on the train from Holyhead most of the day and out of touch with media reports. She was on the last lap of her journey home to Malvern, a few stops down the line from the station to which I was headed.

* * *

BEFORE I RETURNED TO DUBLIN, Dr Samuel Poyntz, the Bishop of Connor, had already announced that he would ordain Connor's two woman deacons, Kathleen Young and Irene Templeton, along with his male deacons on 24 June, just five weeks hence. We rejoiced especially for Irene Templeton, who as Irene McCutcheon had suffered such distress and disappointment at another Synod less than ten years before. Because of the training she had already received, Irene, now married and the mother of a small boy, had been able to take a 'fast route' to ordi-

---

3. The exact figures were: Clergy: For, 126; Against, 55 (69.6% in favour); Laity: For, 172; Against, 29 (86% in favour).

nation as a non-stipendiary deacon in conjunction with the Theological College, so by 1990 she had already served the required year as a deacon in Jordanstown, her parish in Belfast.

I went North for the ordinations, of course, as staff of the college were in any case expected to do. After the impressive afternoon ceremony, and much flashing of press and private cameras, Kathleen went off to celebrate her first service of Holy Communion in her parish, while many of us went home with Irene to celebrate there in a different but equally joyful fashion along with her husband Alan Templeton. Both these Belfast trail-blazers went on to highly successful ministries, Kathleen Young being the first woman in the Church of Ireland to be appointed rector,[4] subsequently being made a canon of Belfast cathedral. Sadly Irene Templeton, who was greatly appreciated in Jordanstown and an inspiration to a whole generation of women ordained as auxiliary ministers, died prematurely from cancer in 1995.

There clearly was no hope that I too would be ordained 'along with the men' in Dublin. Archbishop Caird could not help being hesitant as to how he would handle my ordination, having the feelings of Dean Paterson and some other members of the Concerned Clergy group to consider as well as his own anxieties about our being out of step with the Church of England, which had yet to start its synodical process in this area. 'Do you realise that by ordaining you I shall put myself out of communion with the Bishop of Chichester?'[5] he enquired as we sat together in his study to consult about the matter that summer.

The summer months passed without a decision, although I had suggested that the Feast of St Michael and All Angels, at the end of September, might prove an auspicious time, especially since this would mean that I could start the new academic year in the Theological College with the *fait accompli* of already being a priest. Unfortunately this did not suit the archbishop, since the date happened to coincide with the 40th anniversary of his own

---

4. She was appointed in the autumn of 1992 to St Paul's and St Barnabas, on the northern margins of Belfast's inner city and made a Canon of Belfast Cathedral in 2000.
5. The Bishop of Chichester, the Rt Revd Eric Kemp, was an outspoken and entrenched opponent of the ordination of women at the time.

ordination; so it came about that it was Janet Catterall of Cork diocese, who had been made deacon in England the previous year, who in late September came to be the third woman to be priested in the Church of Ireland. Eventually Dr Caird proposed Sunday 21 October for the big day in Christ Church Cathedral. This was a date which had a particular significance for me, being the day after the eighth anniversary of my husband's death.

My acceptance of the date meant that the staff and students in the college were very much a part of the run-up to the ordination. Perhaps this was not such a bad thing, suggested the Principal, Professor John Bartlett, as some of the emotions on both sides could be acknowledged and even explored. Also, it meant that we could have a party at the college for whoever I wanted to invite on the evening of the ordination.

I was grateful for the party when the time came, but the only 'exploration' I recall is the visit of two of the student opponents of women's priesthood, who asked for a word with me a week or so before the big day. They hoped I knew there was nothing personal to me in their attitude, said Rupert Moreton and Simon Walls, both beginning their 2nd year, but they would not in conscience be able to receive communion from me when I celebrated in the college chapel. What would I like them to do? They could either absent themselves or attend without receiving.

My answer was easily given. Confident that with time it would become clear to them that eucharistic celebration by a woman was both valid and effective, I preferred that they attend. Reception of communion is always optional in any case, I pointed out, so I would never hold their decision not to receive against them. The students were faithful to this agreement for the rest of their time in Braemor Park, and so was I; but to my disappointment, they never changed their minds.

Aware of Dean Paterson's anxiety about the rift that women's ordination was likely to cause with the Roman Catholic Church, I invited all the senior Roman Catholic clergy I knew to the ordination, and found to my delight that they were extremely happy to attend. The Abbot of Glenstal, Dom Celestine Cullen came, along with his confrère Dom Henry O'Shea, my spiritual adviser Fr Eltin Griffin O Carm came from Gort Muire, the Carmelite congregation up the hill from

Braemor Park, Fr Declan Deane SJ my mentor in Buddhist doctrine at the ISE came, as did Fr Austin Flannery OP, editor of
Doctrine and Life.[6] Added to these I was told that Prof Enda
McDonagh from Maynooth and the entire editorial board of *The
Furrow*[7] came to witness the event, along with many women
from the Roman Catholic convents around Dublin. The irony
was that John Paterson himself did not attend. No doubt he
supervised the printing of the ordination ceremony, but a prior
engagement for a Harvest Thanksgiving in the West of Ireland
meant that he was absent.

The major celebrant, of course, was the archbishop; but so
many reservations and caveats about women's ordination were
still being voiced by the opposition that I began to worry that it
might be claimed at some future date that the ordination was in-
valid, there being some deficit of 'intention' on the part of the
archbishop. For this reason I contacted two bishops I knew to be
whole-heartedly in support of my ordination, John Neill and the
former Archbishop of Dublin, Harry McAdoo, to ask if they
could arrange to be present to lay hands on me along with Dr
Caird, and with his permission. And so it came about that with
no less than three pairs of episcopal hands on my head at the
critical point of the rite, as well as those of all Anglican priests
present, there could be absolutely no doubt that I had been ordained into the historic ministry of the church.

The ordination ceremony itself was strangely moving.
Escorted down the aisle by the Archdeacon of Dublin, Gordon
Linney, I seemed to be riding a flood of goodwill and delight
which I knew was not for me personally but for me as a symbol
of all the women who would in future minister in the church.
However unsatisfactory my own ministry might turn out to be,
it was the beginning of the ministry of all the women who
would be ordained in this cathedral in the years to come. I was
at once more and less than myself; I was the symbol of the fulfilment of so many hopes and struggles in my own church and
elsewhere. Hopefully this might prove to be the beginning of a
full ecclesial ministry for women in a much wider arena than the

---

6. The journal of the Dominican Order in Ireland.
7. A journal run from St Patrick's College, the national Roman Catholic
Seminary at Maynooth.

Church of Ireland.

Diana McClatchey had turned up, representing MOW and the Diocese of Worcester, and sat beaming near the front. 'All these people crammed into the cathedral, just for Ginnie!' she exclaimed to her neighbour. And indeed the fact that I was the only person being ordained that day did add something very special to the occasion for us all.

There was a clear rule against photography of any kind in the course of the ceremony; but as soon as the final procession took off all the press photographers and the RTE news cameras flew into action, unfortunately with embarrassing results for some of my Roman Catholic supporters. 'No, my presence at the service was not a statement of support for women's ordination. I was there as a personal friend of Mrs Kennerley,' claimed one of them, caught by a persistent reporter from RTE, and no doubt many of them had 'questions to answer'.

What delighted me more than any of these worthy invitees, however, was the sudden glimpse as I emerged from the cathedral of Fr Romuald Dodd OP, who had been the 'station priest' at RTÉ when my husband first arrived there. I had not seen Rommie since he spoke at Peter's funeral eight years before, and had not thought to contact him; but this was the man who had been so kind to us both from our arrival at the station in the late 1960s up to Peter's illness and death in 1982. And he had come unbidden to see me ordained! Our embrace on that occasion was caught by the *Irish Times* photographer, Ray McManus, and has gone down as an iconic image of that day. To my regret I heard years later that the photo had got Rommie into trouble, though I would be surprised if he had not taken the rebuke in his stride.

In Bray, I was given a great reception the following Sunday, with the presentation of a portable communion set, and glasses of wine, nibbles and speeches at the back of the church after my first parish celebration. It was humbling to receive the support and witness the delight of so many faithful members of the Church of Ireland. One of them had written before the crucial vote to the *Church of Ireland Gazette* as follows:

Have the members of the AAM[8] taken leave of their senses or have they got time on their hands to worry about women priests? Why don't they start thinking about what makes people not go to church? Can they preach good sermons? Do they visit parishioners? Or do they run the parish as if it was their little PLC and they were Chief Executive? Surely a woman priest can do a job as good as any man, as we here in Bray know ... Why not an advertisement promoting the appointment of Women Priests? The present set up is like the male versus female members of a Golf Club.[9]

* * *

THE OPPOSITION, despite the official disbanding of the Concerned Clergy after the 1990 Synod, had 'not gone away, you know', to quote Gerry Adams from another context. Within the Theological College, the Vice-Principal Dr Maurice Stewart encouraged a group of students in their anxiety that they would be discriminated against in their future careers if they could not accept the ministry of women. On the wider scene, a number of senior clergymen held meetings with the Primate, Dr Robin Eames, and John Neill, asking that they deliver on their promise of pastoral care and consideration for the 'minority'. The aim appeared to be to persuade the bishops to introduce a type of 'conscience clause' which would be written into the constitution of the church, to the effect that recognition of the priesthood of women would remain optional for male clergy *in perpetuam*.

Alarm bells rang furiously. It was fair enough for serving clergy to protect their prospects of promotion, but if the *future* clergy were to be encouraged to refuse to serve alongside women, this could be the beginning of the serious split in the church which we thought had been avoided. Yet the proposal put before the 1991 General Synod in the names of the Bishop of Tuam and the Very Revd J. T. F. Paterson was all too clear: that those who objected to the ordination of women 'should suffer no discrimination or loss of respect in their membership or in their ministry by reason of their *bona fide* views nor should such views constitute any impediment to the exercise of ministry in the

8. Association for the Apostolic Ministry, an English group opposed to women's ordination.
9. Joseph A Whitten, Bray, in the *Church of Ireland Gazette*, April 1990.

Church of Ireland'.[10] Immediately one could imagine the House of Bishops becoming divided into those who would and would not ordain women; and we had already in my own case witnessed the embarrassment caused by the dean being 'unable' to be present at the ordination of a woman. Was this sort of difficulty to continue indefinitely? There was also the question of the views of those accepted in future for training for the ministry. Surely they had to accept that they were to be ordained into a church in which an increasing number of their colleagues in the ministry would be women? And surely parish nominators must be allowed to question potential rectors about their willingness to work alongside women, if this is important in their parish?

After consulting with WMG members, many of whom were as alarmed as I was, I first wrote expressing serious concern at the statement to the Primate, Dr Eames, and to Bishops John Neill and Walton Empey, none of whose replies gave me much cause for comfort. Bishop Empey even asserted that he had evidence of 'a witch-hunt on for those opposed to women's ordination'. I also consulted Michael Kennedy, whose experience of General Synod procedure was invaluable, and he replied that the worst danger was that the Bishops' Statement, if 'affirmed' by Synod, might indeed, by way of a further amendment, come to be written with lasting effect into the formularies of the church. Such an amendment he would resolutely oppose. He felt, though, that so long as the hortatory *should* remained in the statement, rather than a mandatory *shall* referring to the lack of discrimination it urged, the effect of the statement itself would not be too seriously harmful. Perhaps we should be generous and let it go.

Not entirely convinced, a position in which I was supported by another old hand at the Synods, WMG member Frank Luce, I rang Canon Cecil Cooper, the editor of the *Church of Ireland Gazette*, to ask would he be willing to publish an editorial from me on the subject. The advantage of this move was that editorials were never signed, so in theory no one but Cecil and I would know who had written it. To my delight he accepted, and I wrote a strong article casting doubt on the wisdom of 'affirming'

10. General Synod 1991. Motion 3. *Recognition of diversities of conviction of faithful members of the Church of Ireland.*

a statement which could make the recognition of women clergy by their colleagues permanently optional. The editorial was run a few days before the opening of the Synod in Belfast. Whether it was needed or not is anybody's guess; but in effect the same arguments were urged on the floor of the Synod. The house by a resounding majority refused to 'affirm' the motion, which was only 'noted and received'.

The Primate was clearly not best pleased, but we could live with that. The sad thing was that John Paterson was so upset that he resigned as one of the honorary secretaries of the Synod. I wrote to him, regretting his decision and assuring him of my personal respect for his views. He had always treated me with courtesy and indeed was always to continue to do so, even welcoming me as a canon of Christ Church Cathedral some five years later. Nonetheless, the measure he had pushed to ensure that the promotion prospects of 'conscientious objectors' would never be affected by their views had to be resisted at all costs. In any case, it was not necessary. Two members of the Concerned Clergy, Ken Clarke and Peter Barrett, were to become bishops in due course, and Maurice Stewart was soon to become Dean of St Patrick's Cathedral in Dublin.

* * *

THE OTHER ATTEMPT to resist the 1990 decision of the General Synod was that of a small group in the North of Ireland who called themselves 'The Church of Ireland, Traditional Rite'. Unable to find any authoritative support within the Church of Ireland, they had found it in a retired bishop from Bermuda, Anselm Genders, and an American bishop of 'The Traditional Anglican Communion', Louis Falk. Although they ordained two priests, it was clear that these had not been appropriately trained – one was a prison officer who had received some training as a lay reader, and the other a member of a traditionalist Anglo-Irish family who was resident in Japan. The group struggled on for a little while, but the numbers were always very small. The only related group is to be found in the Orthodox Church near Stradbally, Co Laois, linked with members of the Cosby family opposed to women's ordination.

And so it was that the Church of Ireland slipped with relative comfort into the acceptance of women in the priesthood of the church. From 1990 on, and more confidently after 1991, it was accepted that women would be part of the ministry of the church. Sheila Zietsman was ordained deacon in the summer of 1990, and put immediately in charge of the parish of Geashill under his own supervision by Bishop Walton Empey; and Martha Gray-Stack, ordained for the auxiliary ministry in Limerick Cathedral the same year, was soon put in charge of the parish of Clara in Co Offaly, under the supervision of the archdeacon, Alastair Grimason.

Perhaps more important was the fact that an increasing number of women were offering and being accepted for training for the stipendiary ministry. By 1992 this reached a peak, with six women and six men entering training in the Theological College. This was also the year when, as already mentioned, Kathleen Young became the first female rector, when she was appointed to St Paul and St Barnabas in Belfast.

CHAPTER TEN

The Women's Ministry Group's Work continues

Serving women both lay and ordained

THE 1990 vote was something of a watershed for the Women's Ministry Group. Our *raison d'être* from the beginning had been to further the full contribution of women to the life and ministry of the church. While we specified that this included both the lay and ordained ministries of women, we nonetheless had put most of our energy into the promotion of women's priesthood. Now that was achieved, we had to reconsider our aims and our role.

One of our first duties, we decided, would now be to offer moral support to ordained women and in particular to exert whatever pressure might be needed to ensure that they received a fair deal from the church administration in terms of pension rights and provision for maternity leave and part-time work while rearing small children. Nor would motherhood be the only difficulty for them; childless or single women could have particular problems in terms of living alone in a tied house, or dovetailing their ministry with their husband's work, with care of an elderly relative, or even of facilitating a relationship with a boyfriend or fiancé.

It was agreed at an early meeting that I would contact Bishop Neill with the request that the WMG be represented on the Committee on the Ordained Ministry, which was being set up on the recommendation of the Select Committee on the Ordination of Women. This I did, but without success. The sometimes rigid structures of the church decreed otherwise. In the nature of such things, this was to be a Committee of the Standing Committee, which meant that all members had to be assigned from the ranks of the Standing Committee, with no seats allotted for co-optees (though there were co-options later to the Commission on Ministry, which succeeded the Committee).

However, Bishop Neill agreed that the WMG should have some input to the Committee, and to this end suggested that we conduct some research the following year among recently ordained women, and report on their experience and their needs. So it came about that we organised a Conference at the Theological College for women clergy, their rectors and if appropriate their husbands in June 1992. Careful notes were taken, checked and if necessary amended by the participants, and forwarded to the Committee on Ordained Ministry with the caution that the material would remain confidential to its members.

The report provided a snapshot of the issues that had arisen for the attendees up to that time, and to that end it is summarised here, with permission from the participants as far as it has been possible to contact them:

The consultation aimed to monitor the experience of parish work of the ordained women in the Church of Ireland, which in the same month [June 1992] reached a dozen. We were particularly interested in the experience of women with family commitments, since we are aware that the arrival of family women in the parochial ministry challenged old assumptions (arguably outdated equally for men) about clerical family life and required the development of new patterns of ministry and deployment and greater flexibility of working conditions.

Attendance

All ordained women were invited, also those to be ordained later in the month and representatives of the women students in the Theological College; husbands and supervising clergy were invited to support them. Eight of the twelve women ordained at this time attended, supported by eight clergy and three husbands. The House of Bishops' link bishop with the WMG, the Rt Revd John Neill, attended as an observer at his own request.

The attendance was as follows:

The Revd Janet Catterall, diocesan youth adviser for Cork Cloyne and Ross, supported by the Rt Revd Roy Warke and the Revd David Catterall;

The Revd Katharine Poulton, curate of Seagoe, and her rector, the Revd David Chillingworth;

The Revd Irene Templeton, non-stipendiary curate of

Jordanstown, with her former rector, the Revd Alex Cheevers and her present one, the Revd E. J. Moore.

The Revd Martha Gray-Stack, auxiliary minister at Limerick Cathedral, with the Very Revd Maurice Sirr;

The Revd Phyllis Fleury, auxiliary minister in Raphoe diocese, with the Very Revd Stephen White;

The Revd Jacqueline Mould, curate of St Aidan's, Belfast, with the Revd W. R. Kelly;

The Revd Margaret Gilbert, awaiting ordination for the parish of Clontarf, with the Revd Tom Haskins and Mr George Gilbert.

Two students from the College, Mrs Frances Bach and Mrs Paula Halliday, accompanied by the Revd Chris Halliday.

The Revd Ginnie Kennerley, Christ Church, Bray and the Theological College, organiser for the WMG.

Suggested topics for discussion had been circulated before the meeting, and of these the meeting elected first to discuss the central areas of *deployment, remuneration, housing, re-deployment* and *timetabling* of parish work for clergywomen with family ties. The procedure was for each woman to describe her situation and recommendations in dialogue with her supporters.

Katharine Poulton and her husband were lucky enough on ordination to find curacies close to each other in the Bangor area; but when Ian Poulton was instituted to the incumbency of a parish in South Down in 1989 there were no openings for Katharine in that area. She continued to commute to Bangor from Downpatrick (around 40 miles) until late in her pregnancy in autumn 1990, when she took the statutory maternity leave, plus a further three months of unpaid leave.

When she took on the curacy of Seagoe in 1991 (45 miles from home) she and her rector were able to work out a system of 38 hours a week plus alternate 'long' and 'short' Sundays for her which both found acceptable. The issues which they felt the church should consider most carefully were as follows:

1. Maternity leave: Can a guideline for clergy and select vestries be provided as to how maternity leave should be arranged? Among the questions requiring attention are the implementation of basic state provisions, the question of continuing help with car loans during the leave period, and the maximum period of leave allowable.

2. Deployment of married couples

a) Should travelling expenses be provided for a person not residing in the 'free house' and travelling a considerable distance to work in the parish?

b) How can working hours best be arranged for those with young children?

c) How can the difficulty of the non-resident cleric's inability to offer 'emergency cover' and to share in the 24-hour life of the community best be addressed?

d) Could part-time work be offered to those with family commitments? If so, how would pension arrangements be adjusted?

e) Could clergy be offered a career break for child-rearing with a subsequent return to full-time ministry?

f) Parishes need to provide space for the non-resident clergywoman (or clergyman) where office work and interviews can take place.

Jacqueline Mould, ordained in June 1991 along with her husband, Jeremy Mould, and priested in June 1992, had so far had little difficulty regarding deployment. The couple lived in her parish, St Aidan's in Sandy Row, and her husband commuted the six miles to Mossley, going there most mornings, returning home for lunch and afternoon preparation work, then returning several evenings a week for parish activites. As the distance was small, he had no sense of being isolated from Mossley, although he had no personal base there. The Moulds were considering the possibility of working in the same parish in the future, perhaps in a job-sharing scheme.

Janet Catterall, mother of three, worked as a part-time parish worker before her ordination to the diaconate in England, and since coming to Ireland had been employed part-time in parish or youth ministry on part stipend – currently 70% of a first year curate's stipend, with her travel but no other expenses reimbursed. She was happy to be offered employment in the same area as her husband, who was rector of Dunmanway, although her job as diocesan youth adviser now took her all over the diocese. Her last child was born in Ireland, and the diocese paid her stipend for a few months until she was ready to return to work. She hoped to work full-time in the future, if possible as rector of a parish not far from her husband's. At this time, she had no objection to fulfilling clergy wife expectations in terms of tray-bakes, MU attendance, etc.

Some discussion ensued as to whether parishioner expect-ations in this area should be encouraged or challenged. The meeting tended to the view that expectations must change with the times, and were already doing so.

Irene Templeton was clearly one of the busiest of the auxiliary priests. Married to a teacher and with a small boy who recently started school, she averaged up to 28 hours work a week for Jordanstown. Outside her parish work, she saw herself as 'a housewife', and said this gave her the flexibility to make herself available at short notice; on the other hand, it could easily lead her into serious overwork. During the vacancy at Seymour Hill in early 1991 she worked full-time for four months. 'It was only tolerable for Alan because the end was in sight,' she said. Irene received no stipend for working hours which would be consid-ered 'full-time' in some professions, but was not discontented on this account, since she considered her expenses payments 'very generous'. Her journey from home to the parish took 25 minutes on weekdays and about half that on Sundays.

Martha Gray-Stack, attached to Limerick Cathedral as an auxil-iary since her ordination in 1990, was a clergy widow with long experience of parish life. She made herself available for duty most of the time, and held the positions of warden of lay readers and chaplain to the Regional Maternity Hospital. She found living in the parish, in widows' housing, to be a great advantage. She was taking weekday services regularly and 'taking up the slack' in the Dean's work, moving into the deanery to cope with whatever oc-curred when he was away. Remuneration was of little concern to her, and she was inclined to think that if she became financially demanding her services would quickly be dispensed with. She did not feel exploited because she loved the work.

Phyllis Fleury, an auxiliary minister with a roving brief in rural Co Donegal, was the participant experiencing the most se-rious problems in her deployment. Sunday duty requiring her to be on the road and conducting services from 8am to 3pm with nowhere in the area open for lunch, was clearly unsatisfactory, especially for a woman around retirement age, as was the heavy mileage required for even one weekday house call. Her case illustrated the importance of carefully assessing deployment issues before auxiliary candidates are recommended for attendance at a Selection Conference.

Finally the meeting considered the experience of the convenor, *Ginnie Kennerley*, working simultaneously as auxiliary curate in Bray and as lecturer in Applied Theology at the CITC. The Bishop of Tuam interposed: 'Mrs Kennerley's situation illustrates perfectly the contradictions the church has got into by not considering these questions carefully enough in advance. She is officially an auxiliary clergywomen working in a stipendiary position and paid as a lay person!' Her worst problem, she said, was that there were not enough hours in the day to do both jobs as she would like. This is a situation which many auxiliary clergy working in the professions would share.

All those present declared themselves pleased with their reception in their parishes, although a small minority of individuals, often clergy, had been slow to accept them. Another comment was that clergy wives of the old school tended to find women clergy hard to accept.

The question of job-sharing or part-time stipendiary work – surely necessary if auxiliaries are to work in the region of 30 hours a week – was discussed, as were the pension adjustments that would be required. The importance of increased flexibility in our structures to meet new conditions was agreed.

It was rewarding to see the fruit of this submission appear in the Report of the Committee on Ordained Ministry eighteen months after its submission.[1] The WMG Consultation was noted as one of the documents referred to in the Committee's deliberations. More important, the major areas we had noted as requiring attention were discussed in some detail, and some legislation suggested. Maternity leave, the development of part-time stipendiary ministries, pension rights related to periods of part-time work, and the need for increased flexibility in our structures were all covered. And the legislation was to follow in due course.

However one area we were less than pleased with came under the heading *Husband/Wife Ministries*.[2] Around 25% of

---

1. In Appendix C of the Standing Committee section of the General Synod 1994 Book of Reports, p 109.
2. p 101 of the 1994 Book of Reports

women clergy tend in general to be married to fellow clergy, as was then and still is the case in the Church of Ireland; and the bar proposed on their sharing ministry in the same parish, as well as the insistence on the requirement of residency in one's own parish and the inadvisability of husband and wife each holding incumbencies, has continued to cause difficulty, or at least anxiety, for clergy couples.

A number of them have shown since then that the anxiety was unnecessary,[3] but the church has been somewhat slow to learn this lesson. While it is certainly true that no cleric, male or female, has the 'right' to a position geographically close to their clergy spouse, most clergy couples have managed with diocesan co-operation to find a reasonable working solution and have been well received *as* couples; but creative possibilities for joint ministry have been missed. Sadly, there has also been a case of marriage breakdown of a couple kept apart by church structures for too long; and another couple is lucky to have survived as a couple given the eight-year separation which they had to endure. Given that other churches of the Anglican Communion have had successful joint ministries of job-sharing co-rectors, it seems unfortunate that the Church of Ireland is not more open to the shared ministry of a husband and wife within a parish.

But this is a lapse into editorialising. The story of the WMG years after the big decision calls us back. As well as continuing to be alert to the needs of women clergy during this time of adjustment in the church, we did our best to widen our support and our focus over a larger area. We spent time as individuals with any women who contacted us personally to discuss their sense of vocation to ordination; and I recall a number of such occasions in my kitchen in Dalkey, often preludes to acceptance at CACTM, theological study and ordination. And as a group we continued with our ministry of both spiritual and material hos-

---

3. For instance the Revds Michael and Ann Wooderson successfully ran adjoining parishes (Naas and Celbridge) in adjoining dioceses from 1998-2006, using both rectories as their joint residence; the Revds Ted Woods and Anne Taylor, who married after she had been working as his curate for some time, still continue in the same parish ministry in Dublin Diocese many years after their marriage; and the Revds Jacqueline and Jeremy Mould are joint curates of Belvoir in the Diocese of Down and Dromore.

pitality, hosting winter Quiet Days and summer parties (the latter partly to replenish our funds).

Then with the Church of England decision on women's priesthood set for November 1992, the international aspect of our activities grew – especially across the Irish Sea. Not only the Church of England, but the Episcopal Church in Scotland and the Church in Wales were gearing up to vote on the ordination of women. The opposition in England in particular was much fiercer, a lot less well-mannered, and far more divisive than it had been in Ireland. At times one felt the Mother Church of the Anglican Communion was tearing itself to bits; and sadly the legacy of the bitter struggle has continued in the 'Flying Bishops' of the Church of England, offering 'alternative episcopal oversight' to those who cannot bear to countenance the sight of a woman on the altar.

There was not a lot most of us could do but pray and keep alert for the news, which we did; but sometimes we might be visiting across the water and on such occasions members of MOW would ask us to speak to groups in their own localities, or to preach in their parish churches. I did so on one occasion for Diana McClatchey in Malvern when on a family visit nearby. The WMG minutes of 1992 have constant references to the upcoming vote in the English Synod, and there is still a letter on file which I wrote to Caroline Davies, then moderator of MOW, in late October, assuring her that we and many more in Ireland were praying for 'a really powerful movement of the Holy Spirit … so that there may be no doubt of God's will in regard to the ordination of women in the Church of England'. We also sent copies of our *Prayers for 1990* to complement the Novenas MOW had distributed to supporters in England and sent to us. It was a great privilege, just sixteen months later, to be invited by the BBC to join in a television programme featuring the ordination to the priesthood of thirty-two women, the first in the Church of England, in Bristol Cathedral.

Another arena for activity was the Ecumenical Forum of European Christian Women, which I had first contacted in the mid-eighties through attending its conference in Finland along with Clare O'Mahony, a colleague on the Glenstal Conference Committee. We continued a relationship with this body, which was headed for some time by our friend in York, Jean Mayland, and occasionally were able to attend its meetings. Early in 1992 we sponsored theological student Nicola Harvey to attend an EFECW Conference in Holland.

There were also a considerable number of invitations to me personally to speak on the Church of Ireland's understanding of women's ministry and its development, mostly from Roman Catholic seminaries such as All Hallows and Milltown Park. The most memorable occasion was the one-day seminar arranged by the ground-breaking new organisation BASIC (Brothers and Sisters in Christ) which my Irish School of Ecumenics colleague Soline Vatinel had founded along with Fr Eamonn McCarthy, to promote the cause of women's ordination in the Roman Catholic Church.[4] It was good to be part of a day for women with a calling to priesthood beyond the confines of our own small church, which even in the Dublin area can only muster 10% of the population.

But of course the WMG's major responsibility was within the Church of Ireland, and during this period we tried equally to support and encourage women in the development of whatever ministries they felt called to without being ordained – in lay reading, pastoral care, healing and hospital ministry, communications, evangelism, teaching or artistic or administrative work, as they felt called. It should be remembered that most members of our committee were lay women and intended to remain so; thus they knew what encouragement women like them needed. And indeed a questionnaire we circulated at the Group's Annual General Meeting in February 1993 confirmed that members wanted more events geared to the needs of women undertaking serious lay ministry in the church, not only within our group but in whatever setting was offered.

A talk I gave to a large Mothers' Union group in South Dublin in May 1993 is an example of the sort of outreach we at-

---

4. The proceedings of the BASIC seminar, with contributions from Mary McAleese, Prof Enda McDonagh, Delma Sheridan, Eamonn McCarthy, Soline Vatinel, myself and a few more, were later published under the title *Women – Sharing Fully in the Ministry of Christ?* Blackwater Press, 1995. Fr Eamonn McCarthy, formerly senior RC chaplain in TCD, was disciplined for his unflinching support for this movement.

tempted. Invited specifically to speak on 'The Ministry of Lay Women in the Church', I suggested that we needed to find a middle way between accepting the church's traditional paternalism with regard to women's 'place' and being swept up in a tide of radical feminism, reacting to the old style of male domination in church affairs. The 'middle way' would be one which saw men and women not so much as divided by their gender as united by their common humanity, remembering that we were created male and female in God's own image and likeness.

All ministry is 'service' (from the Greek *diakonia*); but one can also be too much of a servant – a servant of bossy people rather than of the whole church, taking orders not from God but from those who claim to represent God. We need to learn to trust our own inner authority, the voice of the Spirit within, if we are to help bring in the kingdom of God on earth. The talk went down well, I think; we discussed all manner of options for ministry and ways to prepare for them; and those who were most interested were invited to join us later in the year for an Effectiveness Training Day, led by Ruth Handy of the Irish Management Institute, a woman with a committed involvement in the church.

Despite all this activity, and more, there was a sense in which the WMG was now unsure of its role. Part of the trouble was that there was less interest than we would have hoped from the women ordinands in the Theological College. Even those who initially appeared willing soon began to plead pressure of work, so that eventually we settled to have two of them serve alternately on the Committee, regular attendance being too much for any one. It was disappointing that there seemed to be no new energy for leadership coming into the group, though it was understandable that, the major victory being won, the new recruits just wanted to keep their heads down and get on with the job. It did not help, I am sure, that the average age of WMG members was considerably higher than that of the students; and perhaps my membership of the group put off students who were answerable to me in class.

Daphne Wormell had retired from the WMG chairmanship after the 1990 vote and Jennifer Gill and I had taken on the job between us, while Jane Galbraith had already ceded the secretaryship to Margaret Gilbert. (Both Jane and Margaret were at this point training for the auxiliary ministry and Jane subsequently moved into full-time ministry.) Deciding that the group's purpose and the vision of its members needed to be clarified, Jennifer and I between us compiled a questionnaire to be completed by all at the 1993 AGM. (There were about 20 there, as I recall.) As mentioned above, the result showed a clear demand for more emphasis on women's lay ministries.

We asked members if they wanted the WMG to continue. The answer was a unanimous 'Yes'. We asked if our objective 'to further the full participation of women in the lay and ordained ministries of the Church of Ireland and to support women's ministries in the whole church' was still relevant in 1993. Another unanimous 'Yes'. We asked if any one felt it was time for the WMG to close down? No one was in favour.

Yet inevitably this was the way we were moving. The women coming up for ordination did not seem to need us, and there were other sources of help for those seeking to develop varieties of lay ministry – the Mothers' Union, the Healer Prayer Groups, the Guild of Lay Readers, the various parish and diocesan organisations. The Committee on Ordained Ministry, later to morph into the Commission on Ministry, did not offer us any further outlet or participation in their deliberations. And in addition to all this, we ourselves were getting too busy with our own ministries to continue as before.

Part of my own regular work was directly concerned with the progress of women's ministry in another area: the training of the large crop of ordinands for the non-stipendiary (or auxiliary) ministry, a high proportion of whom were women. Regular study weekends were held for them at the Theological College, and the college staff were roped in for quite a lot of extra teaching, in my case both biblical studies and practical theology. Teaching these mostly middle-aged students was always a pleasure, since they were so enthusiastic, so willing to work and eager to learn. Most of them, women and men alike, became greatly appreciated and indeed indispensable part-time priests in their own localities, and some, such as Olive Henderson and Trevor Lester, went on to successful full-time stipendiary ministry. A few of them, indeed, were clearly brilliant. I remember being startled by the clear 'A+' quality of Maureen Ryan's work

– she was later to become the first woman canon of St Patrick's Cathedral in Dublin, still as a non stipendiary priest. But neither Maureen nor her sisters in the group expressed any serious interest in the WMG. I knew how the suffragettes must have felt after the vote for women was won!

For me, there soon came another factor pointing to the inevitable eclipse of the WMG, in my own life at least. My move late in 1993 from the Theological College into parish ministry 40 miles from Dublin, and the study commitments associated with it (of which more shortly) made it impossible for me to devote as much time and energy to the WMG as before.

So it was no surprise when in November 1994 I received a letter on Women's Ministry Group notepaper from Margaret Gilbert signalling the end of WMG activities. It read in part:

> Following the discussions at the meeting of WMG on November 9th, it was decided that the Group should go into a 'Reflective Mode' and not wind up finally. There will be an annual Quiet Day … to give members an opportunity to meet and greet each other and maintain contact … There was a full and honest dialogue regarding the present support for WMG … In general the members, both present and absent, were in agreement about the way forward, particularly in relation to keeping the structures in place so as to be prepared to act should there be a change of heart among the synods-people of the Church of Ireland about the permanence of the legality of the ordination of women to the priesthood and episcopate.

Effectively, this meant that the Women's Ministry Group recognised that, emergencies excepted, it had outlived its usefulness, and without quite having the courage to announce its own demise, it was prepared quietly to fade away. I think the decision was the right one. Having been such an effective and influential group in the time which gave rise to it, it was fitting that, having done its job, it should free its members for new horizons. The Quiet Day held at the end of that year was effectively the WMG's swansong.

CHAPTER ELEVEN

Transferring to Parish Ministry

Negotiations and more history-making

A T THE END of each academic year I spent teaching at the Theological College I heaved a sigh of relief, enjoyed the prospect of three months of more or less 'normal' lifestyle and enhanced parish activity, and reckoned I could manage just one more year in the place. By Christmas, I was swearing that this would be my last year on the job.

It was not an easy billet. Although I had been offered the usual tied house with the position, I had declined, preferring to continue to enjoy my home in Dalkey on the southern tip of Dublin Bay, at least at weekends. It soon became clear that getting to college from home by 7.30am for Morning Prayer was not, for me, a sustainable option; so I soon negotiated a small bedroom and bathroom on the premises, in quarters known as 'The Bishop's Suite', though they were more akin to an anchorite's cell. But I had no complaints about their size. I was cosy and undisturbed all night in my eyrie high above the chapel on one side and the dining-room on the other.

Daytime was a different matter. From 7.30am through to 9.30pm, one was never out of earshot of the college community. Chapel, breakfast, classes, meetings, private consultations, telephone calls, more meals, more chapel – maybe just the relief of driving in to a lecture in Trinity. Even in the library or walking the dog one was open to interruption. After a couple of years, having started out as a moderately balanced extrovert, I came out as a pronounced introvert on the Myers Briggs personality scale when I investigated it on behalf of the students. I desperately craved time to myself.

But the call to parish ministry amounted to more than that. Bray had offered me the opportunities for real pastoral ministry that I failed to find at the college. Even intellectually it was rewarding. The Monday Club I founded there, promising 'No questions barred', continued for over three years on three Mondays a month almost without summer breaks. 'Pulling the Bible to pieces,' one regular attender had exulted, delighted at having permission to question anything from the creation narratives of Genesis to the Virgin Birth and the Second Coming; but over the years this mixed group of rebels, enquirers and formerly unquestioning 'Yes people' had developed both a modicum of Christian knowledge and an increased level of mutual respect.

Preaching and pastoral visiting had been rewarding too. The sense of actually being able to 'comfort the disturbed and disturb the comfortable' whether in the pulpit or the parlour, was so much more satisfying than the two-way challenges of the Theological College; and I found myself longing for the opportunity to foster the spiritual and community life of a parish of my own – to do what, for the past four years, I had been attempting to train others to do.

The transfer to parish ministry was not going to be easy, however. As well as being female, and thus provoking anxiety in the conservative hearts of some parochial nominators, I was still officially 'auxiliary', and the rule was that auxiliary clergy had to do a course of further study before transferring to full-time stipendiary ministry. With eighteen months to go before my five-year contract expired, I wrote to Archbishop Caird asking for guidance. The reply, sent after consultation with the House of Bishops, was not encouraging. I would have to spend a term 'in a college dealing with pastoral training', presumably in the UK, and I would be required to spend three years in a curacy before proceeding to an incumbency.

I wrote a polite letter in response, though inwardly I was fuming. (In fact, looking through my records, I find I wrote two letters, the first of which, threatening resignation if required to study a subject I had been teaching for the past three years and more, I fortunately did not send!) In the more controlled letter, I told Dr Caird that I would very much like to do a further course of study, provided it was not repeating something I had already done, whether as a pupil or a member of the college staff. Could I make an appointment to discuss the matter with him further? I think that at this meeting the archbishop suggested six months study in St Deiniol's Library, a theological retreat and study centre in North Wales, which was not much better.

Pondering further on our conversation, I wrote to him again on 1 June, requesting some flexibility regarding the further training required and attaching a list of theological and pastoral training already received and teaching undertaken. 'I do understand that whatever decision is taken in my regard must be strictly fair. However, as you pointed out yourself, my case is an unusual one in that my theological and pastoral qualifications and experience are considerably more than those of the usual auxiliary minister.' Would the bishops consider allowing me to fulfil the further training requirement by undertaking a Doctorate of Ministry course in Princeton Theological Seminary in the USA, specifically designed for serving clergy and requiring no interruption of their ministry? This was the type of training I believed would be the most valuable, involving as it did continuing reflection on different areas of one's own ministry, and the production of a 40,000-50,000 word report on a specific ministry project.

This time – it may in fact have been my third outing on the House of Bishops agenda – the bishops put their hands up. I heard that one of their number pointed out that I was already better qualified than many full-time clergy and had more than fulfilled all residence requirements at the college. He proposed that no further course of study should be required of me, and that I should be transferred to the stipendiary ministry as soon as I secured a suitable position. The bishops agreed, adding that as to the DMin, if I wished to pursue it on my own initiative, my bishop might assist me with finance and a modicum of study leave at his discretion.

The negotiations had taken the best part of a year, but the outcome could not have been fairer, and I was glad I had stuck to my guns.

The next step, to which I turned my attention once urgent priorities at the college were under control, was to secure a parish appointment of some sort. A curacy, as originally required by the bishops, appeared to be out of the question – (the few that were available were needed for newly ordained deacons) – so it seemed that I needed to aim at a rectorship. Few parishes at this stage had any experience of women clergy and

Archbishop Caird was convinced it would be most unlikely that any parish in the Diocese of Dublin and Glendalough would want me; nor did he have a bishop's curacy – (a parish to which he could nominate directly) – to offer. In no time it was early in 1993 and my contract at the college would be up that September. It was not encouraging that two parishes in the diocese, one in Co Wicklow and one in South County Dublin, both declined to interview me for a vacancy.

Casting about for other possibilities, I wrote to the Bishop of Meath and Kildare, Walton Empey, who had offered great support through all my time at the college, asking if he would consider having me come to 'bat on his team'. He seemed delighted at the idea and suggested that I ask to be considered for Naas, just half an hour's drive to the south-west of Dublin. I did as he suggested, and spent a number of hopeful hours early that summer with the parish nominators there, but they were minded to do a lot more interviewing before they made a decision.

Then unexpectedly a vacancy was declared in the diocese of Glendalough, in the farming area to the west of the Wicklow mountains. That stretch of country was practically unknown to me. In fact it was so unfamiliar that after putting my name forward I had unwittingly turned up in the area, taking a friend from Bray to spend a 'quiet' weekend at Bolton Abbey near Moone. It was only after we arrived that I realised we were in the middle of the parish I had applied for – and it was an unwritten rule that candidates for a parochial position should not show their face in that parish lest they be deemed to be canvassing! We went to church in Kilkea that morning, just outside the parish boundary, where lay reader Olive Henderson was conducting the service and was somewhat embarrassed that 'the Theological College' had turned up.

So far so good. When Olive drove off it was only 11am and I suggested we go down to Castledermot to look at the famous high crosses in an old graveyard there. As we drew up at the gate, we saw a black-cassocked figure with a small bag getting out of a car. 'Hello! How good to see you! Are you coming to the service?' It was another Church of Ireland lay reader, Philip Hendy, who like Olive knew me from the college. The embarrassing truth hit me: the 10th century crosses, originally erected by the monks of an ancient Celtic Abbey, had of course been transferred with the rest of the site to the Church of Ireland in the 16th century. So they were on what might become 'my' territory! But it was too late to run away. Philip would not take 'No' for an answer, so we had to attend the service, me hoping desperately that I would not be recognised by a legally-minded nominator and disqualified.

Shortly after this *faux pas*, I was invited to meet the nominators of 'Narraghmore and Timolin with Castledermot and Kinneagh' and drove down one wet summer afternoon, splashing my way through pot-holes on what was then a very bad road south from Naas. Two of the four nominators, Ken Ashmore and Charlie Wynne, both of Castledermot and Kinneagh, met me on the spot where Philip Hendy had welcomed me only days before. They showed me round the two southern churches, filling me in on parish problems and controversies as we went. Then as we moved north we were joined by Arthur Keppel of Timolin and Don Ashmore of Narraghmore. As well as each of the four churches, the halls at Castledermot and Timolin had to be inspected, along with the tiny classroom of the one-teacher school in Timolin and then finally the half built Rectory. As we went from one to the other I was quizzed on my ideas for the parish, my attitude to everything from church music to fund-raising, from school activities to the length of sermons – and most important of all, how to keep the parishioners allied to each of the four churches in the parish feeling valued and well catered for.

The parishioners had had a difficult enough time of late. The parish was an amalgamation of the two northernmost churches, which for more than twenty years had been in the care of a popular and devoted pastor, Arthur Jackson, with the two lying to the south of them, almost in the next diocese. When Mr Jackson had left, they had somehow appointed a successor without having suitable accommodation for him, being in the process of selling the two rectories of the former two parishes, before they could buy a site for a new one. The result had been less than happy, the new man living in temporary accommodation first at one edge of the parish and then the other, his health and his patience waning simultaneously, until he resigned only eighteen months or so later, leaving the parishioners feeling disconsolate and hard done by.

I had been warned by the diocesan secretary, Keith Dungan, that I would really need to sell myself and not be too modest, so I spoke quite forthrightly about what I saw as needed for the future well-being of the parish. Attractive worship, good communication, enjoyable social occasions, some lively child-centred activities, and a team of committed parishioners to advise me and help with some of the administrative detail. I also offered them video-recordings of a 'Night Light' series I had recently done for RTÉ, and a television service at which I had spoken, and a tape of some devotional talks for the same organisation. As we looked around the shell of the future rectory, one of their number asked my opinion about its layout and the colour-scheme I would suggest!

That was an encouraging straw in the wind; but I wasn't expecting any early decision. The archbishop had warned me that it would probably be September before the parish made up its mind, and he clearly thought it most unlikely that a farming community would appoint a woman. As a result, the College Principal, John Bartlett, was expecting me back on a temporary extension of my contract for the coming year. I put the matter out of my mind and concentrated on immediate tasks, the first of which was acting as one of the interviewers at the summer Selection Conference for those recommended by their bishops as likely recruits to the ordained ministry.

The selectors were closeted for our final meeting of the Conference when there was a commanding knock at the door and a request that I come to the phone. Naturally I declined, asking that a number be left for me to ring at the end of the meeting. 'Oh Mrs Kennerley, it was the archbishop,' said Kathleen from the kitchen, who had taken the call. 'He seemed very anxious to speak with you at once.' And indeed Dr Caird was disappointed when I rang back. The nominators had left him half an hour ago, and he hadn't wanted to let them go without knowing whether I would accept the nomination to Narraghmore. Without the least intention of refusing the invitation, I had great delight in telling him that this was very sudden, and I would like the opportunity to pray about the offer overnight before giving my response.

* * *

WHAT DATE WOULD SUIT for my institution as incumbent of the parish, the Archdeacon of Glendalough, the Ven Cecil Price, wanted to know. At this stage I was honour bound to complete the pre-term practical weeks in late September and early October which I ran for the students of all three years; but there was little point in staying around any longer, to begin a year of lectures and supervision I would not be able to complete. We settled on Friday 23 October, just two days after the third anniversary of my ordination to the priesthood.

Once again, Archbishop Donald Caird would be the celebrant. Once again, it would a first for him, for me, for the diocese, for the country, and for the media. Even more to the point, it was putting a small country parish prominently on the map and so causing much local excitement.

The archbishop's assistant for the occasion, ironically enough, would be John Paterson, the Dean of Christ Church Cathedral who had been unable to attend my ordination. Some years earlier this would have caused me some anxiety; but by now the Dean had shown me a degree of personal acceptance by inviting me to preach in the cathedral and receiving me as his guest in the new Deanery. I knew he would be graciousness itself for the occasion. And there would be plenty of clergy there whose support would be unstinting.

The expensive new rectory would not be ready for the big day, but as it was nearing completion the diocesan regulation requiring its immediate provision was temporarily waived, and a small but comfortable gate lodge rented for me on the western borders of the parish. Although I went to take a look at it when visiting the parish for consultations about the rectory, I did not take up residence until the evening of the institution, feeling it inappropriate to move in even for an overnight before that.

The institution itself was one of the most heady and exhilarating hours of my life – even surpassing the day of my ordination, if that were possible. Walking up the aisle with the archdeacon, I felt as though I was coming home at last. The words of the processional hymn I had chosen, *Praise to the Lord the Almighty the King of Creation*, suddenly acquired particular relevance:

Hast thou not seen
How thy heart's wishes have been
Granted in what he ordaineth ...

Surely this was where I had been headed all the time.

A whole bus load of supporters, as is customary on such occasions, had come from Bray; and there were so many clergy that they seemed to fill almost half the church. The old school hall across the road was packed to the gills, with closed circuit television cameras relaying not just every word, but every sniff, tear, smile and hesitation to those who could not fit into the church. Once again, I was making history. It was a sensation that could properly be described as 'awesome' in the teenage vernacular of the day.

I had invited John Bartlett to preach for the occasion. As well as reflecting on the 'vision' required for parish ministry, I remember him warning every one that wherever I went my dog Sam went too. (Sam was in the car at the gate, as near as he could get for the time being.) My former rector David Godfrey read the gospel; the clergyman from Athy, Leslie Crampton, who had been responsible for organising the service, delivered the Old Testament reading and the school principal from Timolin, Kathleen Keppel, the epistle.

It was an ecumenical and community occasion as well. The local convent opened its school gymnasium for the reception that followed the service, the nuns excited to be hosting the reception for the first woman rector in the Republic. The local parish priest, Fr Michael FitzGerald, was present, and after his speech of welcome presented me with a handsome antique map of the parish area. A number of local TDs, parliamentary representatives from counties Wicklow and Kildare, and a deputation of monks from the Cistercian Bolton Abbey, were out for the occasion, along with the press and many of the local worthies, including Castledermot's two resident gardaí, keeping their eyes peeled to make sure no one got lost between the church and the convent, or obstructed traffic by inappropriate parking. One of the nominators, agricultural merchant Charlie Wynne, took a photo of the three of us as I finally left the church – each of us wearing our own style of peaked cap – a refreshing change from all the ecclesiastical dignitaries of the day, though there were plenty of photos of those too.

The reception in the convent was where I met for the first time many of the women of the parish, pouring tea, passing sandwiches, offering tray-bake delicacies, as the serious business of 'the speeches' got under way and both the press and the amateur photographers got busy recording the occasion. I guess it was on this occasion that I first learned to speak *ex tempore*. There had been no time to write a speech, though I knew one would be required of me. It didn't matter. The words flowed simply out of my joy at having arrived and been accepted, with the support of so many future parishioners, past parishioners and fellow clergy. The rise of the heart each time I had turned down the road from the mountains to the parish, on journeys of exploration and preparation; the warmth of the women who had come to Dublin to help me choose curtains, and the men who had helped me select the kitchen cabinets and make decisions about the landscaping – all flowed in. Never had I been so well cared for in my life.

I think I mentioned also that the whole occasion felt a little bit like a marriage. The parishioners and I were committing ourselves to each other without knowing each other more than superficially. What I knew about farming would fit on the back of a postage stamp, but at least I had been brought up in the countryside and was happy at the thought of returning to the country life. There might be some surprises ahead, but I hoped we were well enough matched that we would learn to live together happily and productively, bringing each other closer to God as we went along.

My friend Margaret Howard had driven down with me earlier in the day with just a couple of suitcases and enough liturgical books and biblical resources, along with the computer, to keep me going for a few weeks. I was glad to have her to return to the gate lodge with me and Sam after we had waved the visitors goodbye and I had said goodnight and thank you to my new parishioners. She was to stay the weekend and return for many weekends more – a fantastic support and prayer partner for my first years in the parish. 'Are you the priest's housekeeper?' some one asked her that weekend at a book launch attended also by the local parish priest. 'No,' said Margaret. 'I'm the other priest's housekeeper'. And so, sometimes, she almost was!

* * *

THERE WAS MUCH TO DO in the first few months in the parish. But more important than any one thing was gaining the confidence and earning the respect of the parishioners. Worship was the place to start, and the first question was the service times in the four churches. Obviously they couldn't all have the prime slot of 11am on Sunday mornings; but no one wanted services as late as noon or as early as 8am.

'What about Sunday evenings?' I enquired of key parishioners in Kinneagh, the tiny church half way to nowhere at the southern end of the parish.

'Oh no. Definitely not. That's when people are visiting their relations.'

'M'mm. All right. Then what about Saturday evening?'

'Saturday evening? Well I suppose we could try it. So long as it wasn't more than once a month.'

And indeed the monthly Saturday evening service in Kinneagh attracted quite a few more than turned out for the 8.30am service; and the parishioners who favoured that church were rewarded with one service a month at their preferred time of 9.45am – after the farmers' yard work was done, but early enough to free them the rest of the day. Each church had its own monthly rota of three Sunday services at different times, leaving its congregation one Sunday free to attend another church in the group.

I was lucky that my predecessor had already dispensed with the 'old' prayer book; lucky also that he had bought a stock of modern hymn-books so that we could have a varied musical diet, (though there were always those who hated, on principle, any hymn they did not know!) On the whole I found that so long as people had three hymns they knew and liked, they would put up with one new one, which sometimes we would rehearse before the service started.

We evolved a Sunday worship system of short communion services at 8.30am, Morning Prayer or Family Services at 9.45am and full length communion services at 11.30am. This gave just enough time for me to greet parishioners in a relaxed way at each church before heading on to the next one, though rarely time for a cup of coffee or an adjustment to the sermon.

Altogether I suppose it was a bit of a culture shock, after being accustomed to serving just one church, to have to fit three services into every Sunday morning, with considerable mileage between each, and so many different church wardens, lesson readers and organists to relate to. I wrote about this in humorous vein for a national newspaper, expressing my shock at finding myself with four churches, eight church wardens, two select vestries (parish councils) two glebe wardens, two parish treasurers, two hon secretaries, and just one of me! I also had one lay-reader, the aforementioned Philip Hendy, who would have been more than willing to 'fly solo' for one service each Sunday, leaving me to do the others; but I decided against this, reckoning that it was important that I be there for the worshippers in each church, both for the conduct of the worship and preaching and to shake their hands at the door and listen to whatever they might have to say.

With the help of Charlie Wynne and the Building Committee, we managed to get the new carpets and the vanload of my furniture, both new and old, into the rectory just in time for Christmas. I have an abiding memory of having to dry out the dining-room floor with an industrial size dehumidifier in early December. (Somehow the window drainage system had been installed back to front.) But by the Sunday night before Christmas, the evening of the traditional Castledermot Carol Service, all was cosy and welcoming in the handsome house that the parish had provided for me.

It was a level of modest luxury I had never aspired to in my own home. It would have been nice to invite friends there for Christmas Day itself; but the thought of catering Christmas dinner after conducting four special services in 24 hours did not really appeal. Nor did going to any one of the parish families who invited me, since this would run the risk of offending all the others.

Luckily invitations from my old home territory were not lacking. Both Daphne Wormell and John and Jan Bartlett asked me for Christmas Day almost routinely for many years. For this first Christmas of my new life in the country, what better than to accept Daphne's invitation to Christmas dinner at her home in Shankill, so close to home that I could stay in Dalkey overnight? Daphne for the rest of her life remained one of my most loyal friends and encouragers. What a lot I and all the rising women clergy owed her.

CHAPTER TWELVE

In the Parish

Challenges — Achievements – and More Challenges

IT WOULD BE impossible to cover my eleven years of ministry in the parish in one chapter. So what will follow will just point to some of the landmarks in the scene of those years. Looked at from the far side of 'retirement' (a word I hate) there were a few major events that gave us all encouragement, especially two in the early days. The first was the Castledermot roof campaign and its happy conclusion; the second was the advent of a second teacher and a second classroom for Timolin School.

The Castledermot church roof had been causing concern for some time; and the rector's church warden there, Mac Brandrick, had recently been up in the rafters with a camera, recording all the worst bits of rot, and had a plan to sell notional 'roof-slates' to any one who would part with a few pounds. A local builder specialising in church roof restoration, Michael O'Regan, warned that we would need at least £25,000 for the job. So my first challenge was clear. How could we raise the funds?

Like most country parishes, Castledermot and Kinneagh (which kept its finances separate and even secret from Narraghmore and Timolin) operated with very little cash to spare. The annual 'sustentation' payments, expected from each family around harvest time, and the church collections were barely enough to keep things turning over, especially since the entire sale price of the Castledermot rectory had been put to the building of the new rectory in Timolin. In fact, without the discos which the parish used to hold in a local hotel each year, the parish would already have been in trouble.

So I reckoned we needed to invite the support of the majority Roman Catholic community around us – (96% of the population) – as well as of fellow members of the Church of Ireland over a wide area. How could we make it enjoyable for them to participate? I considered we had to show the need, offer some heart-warming entertainment and some tangible mementoes of the occasion and, rather than demanding any fixed sum from people, invite them to put cash or cheques into the envelopes that we would provide. Before we asked for anything, each arrival would be offered a glass of wine, hopefully sponsored by some licensed provider. And of course we would invite the archbishop and Mrs Caird down to Kilkea Castle for the occasion.

Given the hard work of an enthusiastic committee and a few personal friends, everything went with a swing. We got going as soon as the Christmas festivities were over. The banqueting manager at the Castle was approached and a date in the spring set. My photographer friend from Bray, Geraldine Urch, came down to take a poetic series of pictures of the church, the famous high crosses, the high tower, the vistas. Together we mounted them on 4' by 3' black boards, decorated and captioned in gold ink, and eventually set them up on screens procured from a local bank in the hotel ballroom. Mac Brandrick's photos of roof decay were set up nearby. My new friend at Timolin's Irish Pewter Mill (on the site once occupied by St Moling and his monks) offered to produce jewellery for the occasion. Pewter crosses, based on the Adam and Eve iconography of Castledermot's North Cross, were designed and made for us at cost price, as brooches, pendants, and pectoral crosses suitable for bishops.

The jewellery sales point was set up near the ballroom entrance, and beside it the 'buy-a-roof-slate' stall, offering certificates of ownership of slates numbered 1-5,000. Refreshments were rustled up by a team of our best caterers, posters got out, wine and glasses got in, and, best of all, a local band was recruited, complete with Sr Teresa from the convent on the violin and a very young Michael English on the keyboard.

We arranged a special pendant to present to Mrs Caird, and Sean Clery at the Pewter Mill asked if we would like one put on a pewter plate for the archbishop.

'How much would that cost?'

'I could do it for twenty-five pounds.'

'No, I don't think so. We're trying to make money, not spend it.'

The Castledermot treasurer, Malcolm Cope agreed.

'Don't worry. I'll get him something he'll enjoy,' he assured me. 'He was our chaplain at school in Portora. I know what he'll like.'

When Malcolm and I took our seats for the speeches on the platform alongside the archbishop, His Grace enquired, 'What's that you've got under your chair, Malcolm?'

'It's a six-pack of Guinness, Your Grace,' came the dead-pan reply. As it turned out, when presentation time came, it was a football supporters' kit for the World Cup soccer match to be played a short time later. The archbishop accepted it with enthusiasm, put on the tricolour cap immediately – (he offered me the muff) – and insisted on wearing it for the rest of the evening, even for the photographs to be published in the Diocesan Review.

That was the occasion on which it became clear that Dr Caird had accepted me and the principle of women's priestly ministry without further reservations. I knew it when instead of addressing me as 'Mrs Kennerley' as he rose to speak, he came out with 'Ginnie'. I was a member of his 'family' at last.

That first big fund-raising event took place only a few days before I took off for Princeton on the second of my short visits in pursuit of my doctorate of ministry – (the first had been the previous September, before my arrival in the parish). When I returned three weeks later, with money from fellow students for Castledermot crosses in my handbag, almost all the money we needed was in – over £18,000 already. 'You've given us new confidence in ourselves,' said Charlie Wynne. 'Everything is possible!' And indeed, that very autumn the archbishop came down for the Harvest Thanksgiving Service to dedicate and bless the new roof..

* * *

THERE WAS A FAR BIGGER challenge at the northern end of the parish. Timolin National School had twenty-eight children aged from four and a half to twelve years, cramped into old-style multiple-occupancy desks facing a couple of large blackboards. The room had been built as an extension of the enlarged parish hall some thirty years before, and had originally been spacious enough for the small numbers, which were down to only seven at one time. Now, with the rising birth rate related to the increased farm incomes of the 1980s, it was seriously over-crowded.

Mrs Keppel, who was both the principal and the sole full-time teacher, was highly experienced, a firm disciplinarian and loved the children, as they loved her (though some of the parents were terrified of her!) She had a little regular help from parents or former parents with art and sport, but otherwise managed to teach all eight classes in the school simultaneously. As rector, I was invited to teach Religious Education, a task which my predecessor had declined, though Mr Jackson had taught the children faithfully and they loved him dearly.

My style as a (totally untrained) teacher was rather different from what the children had experienced before, but I tried to keep to the required syllabus until mercifully a more imaginative one came along. What we all most enjoyed was preparing new songs or little playlets which the children would then present in the occasional family services, with extra special performances at Christmas and the end of the school year. I soon found that whatever I said in class went home with the children, and proved the basis of many a 'theological' discussion with their parents. Not a bad way to get some fresh thinking going!

As rector, I found I was automatically 'chairperson' of the school board, which had responsibility for all decisions concerning the school. Mrs Keppel was the secretary, the treasurer was a farmer whose children had all attended the school, and the number was completed by two parent representatives, Carol Glynn and Robert Ashe, an archbishop's appointee and a community nominee. With this committee I shared my anxiety about the cramped conditions, the difficult teacher-pupil ratio, and my discovery that we actually had just enough pupils to claim the services of a second teacher from the Department of Education.

But where could such a teacher function? Hardly in the lofty and hard-to-heat parish hall to which the school-room was attached. But for the time being there was the parish 'kitchen' beyond it, and a small, damp, unused little room beside it which had once been the sitting-room of the now derelict teacher's residence.

We agreed to make application to the Department at once; and in the meantime one of the parents, a principal teacher on a year's maternity leave, undertook to do a few hours a week to take some of the pressure from Mrs Keppel. While she operated in the kitchen, Carol Glynn got to work in the former sitting-room – stripping out decayed plaster and rotting wood, then polybonding, painting and papering until we had a presentable little space, only about nine foot square, easily heatable, where some teaching could take place until we could contrive something better.

We got our full-time second teacher the following autumn. Yvonne Deacon, from nearby Grange Con, operated for a full year with the smaller children in Carol's reclaimed space, which she somehow made habitable for sixteen children and herself with new desks and chairs funded by the Department, though there was no room for a desk for her own use. For some time after this we had to keep an eagle eye on enrolments, for fear of losing both Yvonne and our hoped-for new schoolroom if pupil numbers dropped below the required figure.

The biggest task was to get funding approved for the brand new school room we needed. My original hope that we could convert the remains of the teacher's residence was quickly dismissed. The concrete walls were crumbling, what passed for a roof was leaking and the whole structure was beyond hope of reclamation. A number of strong letters and determined visits by Robert Ashe and myself to the decision-makers at the Department of Education in Dublin brought us approval for a new structure on the site sooner than I had expected. Almost before we knew it we were showing the Department's architect around the area of weeds, old septic tanks and crumbling masonry behind the parish hall and gearing ourselves to raise the 15% of the budget estimate required of us.

With Carol's help once again, and with Mrs Keppel's old registers in hand, we contacted all the past pupils of the school to invite them to a special evensong in Timolin Church, to be followed by a reception at which we would launch the appeal. Once again there was to be a photo display – pictures going back to the 1920s of former school children and their teachers, gleaned from around the parish, in addition to new photos of the children and teachers of the day. There was also a display of the children's art-work, and as the *pièce de résistance*, with a little adult help, they produced a mural of the Timolin area – church, hall, sexton's cottage, post office, high cross, rectory, Keppels' house, river, main road, and a number of their own homes – which still decorates the hall to this day.

It was a wonderful afternoon, attended by a huge number of past pupils from far and wide, parents, parishioners, local parish priests and clergy, officers of our Diocesan Board of Education, a monk from Bolton Abbey, and most important of all our friendly school inspector Pádraig Ó Loingsigh, whose support had been absolutely invaluable. Inevitably it was not our only fund-raising event. The biggest earner around that time was a 'Dream Auction' a few months later run with fantastic support from parishioners, parents and local well-wishers, chiefly in aid of the restoration of Timolin Church. As with the Castledermot 'roof' evening, I was astonished at how generously people supported an event for a good cause that was also made 'a good night out'.

The formal opening of the new school building, in the autumn of 1996, was for all of us associated with the school a hugely exciting event. The building was blessed by the new Archbishop, Walton Empey; the tape across the doorway from the new playground to the lobby was cut by our local TD, Alan Dukes; there was a service of thanksgiving led by the children in the church hall; there were speeches and photos and refreshments; and of course we had a tree-planting ceremony – as the archbishop dug a willow tree into the swampy ground we planned to make into a nature reserve in the old 'school field'. The archbishop, swathed in his magenta cassock, also took to playing netball with the children on the new playground, crowded as it was with parish families, the press, diocesan dignitaries and local clergy and well-wishers.

Timolin School was reborn, the community clearly 'on the map', as was demonstrated by the new finger-post pointing to both school and church from the main road. But who would have thought that, only a few years later, our school inspector Pádraig Ó Loingsigh would once again be encouraging us to build a new school room? Today the school has two bright modern classrooms, linked by a corridor along the back of the parish hall, and the cramped little classroom I originally found there is used as a library and computer room. If I had to point to one result of my arrival in the parish, it would be that school, which my predecessor had said 'would close as soon as Mrs Keppel retires'. Instead, it was resurrected!

* * *

THESE COMMUNAL ACHIEVEMENTS, the re-roofing of the Castledermot church and the opening of the new school in Timolin, certainly gave a much needed morale-boost to my parishioners, as did the restoration and redecoration of Timolin Church a little later; but that did not mean that the parish could be considered spiritually vibrant or even spiritually healthy. In common with parishes everywhere in a time of rising secularisation, attendance at worship was lower than in previous generations, scepticism about childhood tenets of faith was rising, and religious practice was generally seen as duty rather than as blessing. I knew there could be no simple answer or reversal of such deep-seated attitudes and trends. The first step had to be to understand what was going on and why; only then could one hope to make initiatives which could lead to spiritual renewal of any kind.

From the beginning of my time in the parish, I was spending a number of hours every week on reading, pondering and writing for the doctorate of ministry programme in which I had enrolled in September 1993. In the first two years, I wrote a number of 5,000 word reflections on particular examples of my contact with parishioners, carefully selected so as to give examples of administrative, educational, spiritual and evangelistic initiatives. These reports were circulated to my colleagues on the programme a few weeks before our Princeton meetings in May each year, where we dissected and commented on each other's work along with the staff members responsible for the programme.

At our third meeting, in May 1995, each student was expected to come up with a proposal for a 'Final Project', a piece of research designed to help each participant come to a deeper understanding of a key aspect of their current ministry. After much reflection, I came up with the title, 'The Participation of the

Younger Men in a Country Parish of the Church of Ireland'. The younger men, fathers of young families between the ages of 25 and 35, were the people in the community I found it hardest to get to know. They were shyer than their wives, less likely to be in church, less likely to be in the kitchen if I dropped by to say hello, and, being a woman, I didn't feel I could drop into the pub to chat with them on their own territory. By picking this subject, I would be forcing myself to open up serious dialogue with an important sector of the parish community. The word 'particip-ation' was crucial. There are many ways of participatin in parish life without attending church very frequently, and I wanted to recognise their part in parish life in whatever way they understood it themselves.

The research was done by way of personal interviews with the members of this grouping as well as the older men in the northern part of the parish; also by a written questionnaire given to all adult or confirmed members of the parish. The major re-sults were, I think, indicative of attitudes in most country parishes of the Church of Ireland. They showed clearly that peo-ple valued their 'Protestant' heritage, and that they valued the church chiefly in relation to provision for their children. There were certain local conditions which affected answers one way or another, particularly in relation to the lower participation of the men associated with one of the churches. One of these con-cerned my own gender in relation to the lower church atten-dance of its young men, as I observed:

> The larger age cohort [in this area] of younger men ... asserted their in-dependence and their manhood when they came of age by resisting the matriarchal pressure in this community to attend church, making the pub their community centre instead. It is possible that this resis-tance has been intensified over the past three years by the presence of a female rector – all too easily identified with the not-so-lamented matriarchy of the past generation. It could also be an expression of liberation from the control of the primary school-mistress, who had considerable power over these young men's lives in their early years.[1]

---

1. *Participation of the Younger Men in a Country Parish of the Church of Ireland*, 1998. (Available in the Church of Ireland Representative Church Body Library) p 99.

The general picture that emerged, when I completed the work in the summer of 1997, was fairly bleak:

> a microcosm of a minority community in decline in an increasingly secular society ... [with] a resultant lack of religious vitality, a conservative piety being the option of most of the community's 'religious' people, rather than any life-enhancing celebration of Christian salvation, or any sense of mission beyond community boundaries.[2]

It was not a flattering description of my beloved parish, but I'm afraid, with a few saintly exceptions, it was a fair one. The final chapter of the dissertation sought out 'signs of hope' and 'openings for ministry' which I aimed to pursue for the remainder of my time there, to provide fertile ground for the spiritual renewal I knew to be needed for the church's effectiveness and survival in the new millennium.

It would have been good to see the dissertation published in some form, but because some of the participants would have been too clearly identifiable I did not pursue the idea with any energy. It was mildly gratifying that I was asked to present a digest of the research at the Diocesan Clergy Conference after the degree was awarded, and that the Diocese of Cashel and Ossory also invited me to discuss it at a clergy meeting. For any one who is interested – some have been and I hope more will be – the finished product is available at the Representative Church Body Library in Dublin; and a number of copies were circulated to the archbishops under whom I served and other key figures in the church. It occurs to me now that I should have given one to my successor in the parish. Perhaps it is not too late!

* * *

ONE OF THE SAD THINGS about ordained ministry in the Church of Ireland – and indeed any Christian ministry, I imagine – is that there is simply not time in the day or the week for all the things one feels called to accomplish – such as following up on all the 'openings for ministry' I identified in my Princeton work. Even working 24/7, one cannot hope to make all the visits one should, come up with the best ideas for study or discussion groups, concoct the best sermons or parish

---

2. idem p 113.

newsletters, prepare the best RE lessons, or organise parish worship and social events that are as compelling as one would have them. Time for prayer is never sufficient either.

Add to this the fact that the more one is appreciated by one's bishop, and the more one is respected by the wider church, the less time one will have for parish ministry and we come up with a major problem for clerical effectiveness, whatever the gender of the cleric.

After the Timolin School opening of 1996 I found myself quickly recognised by the wider church in a number of ways: I was voted onto the Diocesan Board of Education, I was appointed to a canonry in Christ Church Cathedral – (to my surprise, with no opposition from the Dean, although I was the first woman canon in the Church of Ireland); then in 1998 I was appointed one of the two rural deans for West Glendalough, and then as clerical secretary for Glendalough of the Diocesan Synods and a member of the Diocesan Board of Nomination and the Councils; and finally I was put in charge of the training and support of the Lay Readers of the Diocese as their Warden. (However, I never quite made it to the General Synod, languishing for years as a 'reserve', which I rather regretted.)

The Board of Education meetings required occasional attendance in Dublin which, given the driving required, took half a day each time; the canonry at the cathedral was not burdensome, involving as it did two Sunday preachments a year followed by two attendances at evensong in the same week; so these appointments did not remove me from the parish more than was compensated for by giving up singing with the Carlow Choral Society. However, taking over the job with the lay readers did cause me to hesitate, given that it required not only monthly meetings of the Guild of Readers but constant interaction with trainee readers and consultations regarding the programme of events. I also wanted to be able realistically to offer hospitality to the readers as a group on at least an annual basis. All this would have been much easier for some one based in Dublin.

However, I loved having both the Lay Reader and the Christ Church Cathedral responsibilities. My occasional work helping to train the auxiliaries and mark their essays for the Theological College had been fading as new systems came into place, so it was good to be back in something of a guiding role with people seriously preparing for ministry. As to the cathedral, where I was to be elected to the Board, the privilege of preaching there regularly was both challenging and exhilarating. In the parish, I had evolved a system of usually preaching three different sermons each Sunday from carefully prepared notes, varying what I said according to the people who turned up to worship in each church and the inspiration of the moment. For the cathedral, I had to have a carefully composed sermon which would read like spontaneous speech and would be thought-provoking and challenging for a very different type of congregation – one which would instantly spot any woolly thinking or naïveté, and which usually included a few distinguished Anglicans from around the world.

* * *

A LOT MORE COULD BE SAID about the highs and lows of parish life and ministry – the highs for me included increased ecumenical activity and co-operation, especially between ourselves and the monks of Bolton Abbey, but also in inter-church services and study groups, and the continuing dramatic and liturgical work with the children, for whom we also organised an ecumenical and 'co-ed' scout troupe, run on our premises but with leaders and children from both church traditions in the locality.

However, in the context of this book it is more appropriate finally to consider what it meant to be the first woman rector in the Republic. It was a few years before country parishes nearby followed suit by appointing women, so apart from the support of my neighbouring rector Leslie Crampton in Athy, I was ploughing a lonely furrow for a while, telephoning my former rector David Godfrey or Archdeacon Edgar Swann for advice whenever I was uncertain of proper procedure.

Things began to change from 1997, when Paula Halliday was appointed to Crosspatrick and Carnew (Diocese of Ferns) and then 1998, when Olive Donohoe was appointed to Mountmellick and Ann Wooderson to Celbridge (both in the Diocese of Meath and Kildare). Nancy Gillespie came to Stradbally in 2000, Stella Durand, under the supervision of the rector of Baltinglass, to

Kiltegan the same year and Lynda Peilow to Edenderry in 2001. The same year, Olive Henderson, ordained as an auxiliary in 1997, had been put in charge of Rathdrum in the Wicklow Mountains; and finally Hilary Dungan was appointed to Portlaoise in 2003. These were just the women appointed within an hour's drive of Timolin; all of them in rural or semi-rural parishes. One can only speculate as to how much their appointment owed to the lack of suitable male applicants, as indeed I had speculated in my own case. Certainly it took longer for parishes in Dublin to appoint women, it being 2004 before Gillian Wharton was appointed to Booterstown and Sonia Gyles to Sandford, although it's true I received some enquiries from Dublin parishes in the late 1990s, as did some of the other women.

It would be nice to be able to say that a good degree of mutual support developed between the new women rectors, but I don't think the 'sisterhood' which the feminist constituency would have hoped for came to pass. The nearest I got to it was in my friendship with Ann Wooderson, whose institution to Celbridge, after four years' frustration looking for a ministry convenient to her husband's parish in Naas, was the first over which I presided as rural dean. On the whole I think the distances between our parishes, the priority we had to give to relationships with our immediately neighbouring fellow clergy, and sheer pressure of work militated against the development of meaningful woman-to-woman support. Whatever such support I received came from lay women, usually friends who visited at weekends, but this was always more domestic than professional support.

Living in a large rectory on my own, I felt it important to share the place with parishioners occasionally, inviting groups for coffee, tea, or even occasionally for dinner, though I drew the line at having select vestry meetings there. But it was also my home and I decided at an early date that I would invite who I wanted when I wanted and not worry about any parish gossip this might cause. As a single woman, I could easily have considered myself so vulnerable to gossip that I would never have had any one to stay, male or female, married or single, old, middle-aged or young. If people want to gossip they will find grounds for gossip anyway. So I did occasionally invite male clergy (often coming to preach for me) or male relations to stay as well as the women friends, sometimes with husbands or sons, who were more regular.

On one such occasion, when my forty-something stepson had come to visit to discuss a family emergency, I sent him up the road to walk the dog. Next day, when I dropped in for coffee with a farmer's wife nearby I was properly quizzed. 'Bernie up the road wants to know who's the canon's toy boy?' she challenged me. If I had allowed such considerations to affect me, it would have been a very lonely life.

Apart from such issues regarding my personal life, and the self-imposed bar already mentioned on going into pubs on my own, I don't really think my gender caused me any problems in the parish, unless the suggestion is correct that some of the younger men identified me somehow with formerly resented matriarchal authority in their lives. My being female may have caused problems for an occasional parishioner, but no more than any rector's personal quirks always cause difficulties for someone.

When it came to leaving the parish, however – and it was said I left it 'in good heart' – I felt it important that the next rector be a man, and if possible a youngish family man. Whatever is lacking in one rector needs to provided in the next one. Similarly, when I was inviting preachers for special services, even the monthly healing services in Castledermot, I would usually make an effort to invite a man, simply because I am in favour of gender balance in ministry. I had nothing to do with the appointment of my successor, of course, but I was and remain delighted at the nominators' choice of Isaac Delamere, a young clergyman with a young family and with strong interchurch connections. He is doing much in the parish that I could never have done; just as I did things that others could not do. No one has all the gifts to minister to every one; and both male and female are needed in the ministry of the church.

CHAPTER THIRTEEN

Celebration and Reflection

Research and the Future of Ministry

I N THE YEAR 2000, two women priests of Dublin Diocese, Anne Taylor and Susan Green, organised a two-day conference in the Theological College, 'Celebrating Ten Years of Women Priests'. They drew up a programme of speakers which included Canon Kenneth Kearon, who was then the Director of the Irish School of Ecumenics, Ann Thurston, a Roman Catholic theologian married to an Anglican, Canon Maureen Ryan of Galway, Rev Katherine Meyer, Presbyterian chaplain at TCD, Una Agnew, lecturer in spirituality at Milltown Park, and myself. Since I was the first and still the only woman canon of Christ Church Cathedral, they also invited me to celebrate the special eucharist which was to open the conference there on Sunday 3 September.

A total of 34 ordained or ordinand women attended the conference, some of them from as far away as Co Antrim. Of these 13 were stipendiary clergy, 13 were non-stipendiaries, 4 were in training for stipendiary ministry and 4 in training as non-stipendiaries. At that time there were 31 full time women clergy serving in the Church of Ireland and 28 non-stipendiaries, amounting to just over 10% of the total number of clergy (500 full-time and 77 auxiliaries). Now, according to the *Church of Ireland Directory* for 2008, there are approximately 61 stipendiary women clergy of whom 31 are rectors, amounting to just over 12% of the 492 clergy on the church's pay roll; there are 39 serving non-stipendiary women out of a total of 113 NSMs – well over a third of the total. Some of the full-time women moved over from auxiliary ministry and some have come here from Anglican churches abroad; but most of the stipendiary intake between 2000 and 2008 entered through the BTh course in the Theological College.[1]

---

1. See Appendix A for complete list of women in ministry according to the *Church of Ireland Directory* for 2008, sorted according to category and date of ordination.

Two things were remarkable about the 10th Anniversary Conference of 2000: the first was that it was the only event since the demise of the WMG six years before that was organised specifically for women in the ordained ministry of the church; the second was that, although it was agreed that we should arrange something similar on an annual or even bi-annual basis, nothing of the same kind has happened since, despite 'the joy, the fun and the support [that] came from simply being together'.[2]

Reading over the report eight years later, the question about the *difference* the ministry of women makes, or should make, returns to me in a more compelling way than before. Twenty-one years on from the ordination of the Church of Ireland's first woman deacon, we are now into the second generation of women clergy in our church. Looking back on the way we of the first generation went about our trail-blazing activities, I think it is clear that most of us, if not all, opted in to the expectations of our ministry formed within the patriarchal structures of our tradition. We needed to show that we could do the job as defined by the tradition of the church and the expectations of the parishes, defining ourselves as human (a dignity which perhaps had been denied us) rather than as female (an identity that was still scorned by too many). We succeeded, despite the expectations of many who did not initially welcome us; but could our ministry have been more transformative if we had been prouder of our gender, if we had had the self-confidence to follow God in 'doing a new thing'? For myself I am not sure, having always thought of myself as primarily human and incidentally female, but it remains a matter worth pondering.

The question is underlined by some thoughts of Ann Thurston, cited in Anne Taylor's Report:[3]

> The ordination of women does not resolve gender issues in the church. Was the vote in 1984 and then in 1990 the end of the story or the beginning of a new story? Nor will the [patriarchal] system change because a few women slip through the room and get to the top.

---

2. 'About this Report', Anne Taylor in *Celebrating 10 Years of Women Priests*, privately produced, Dublin, 2000.
3. op. cit. p 5.

Women have been reluctant to be identified with the F word – feminism. But whereas in the early days there was much anger and negativity, that is not the case now. Feminism could be defined as:

The promotion of the full humanity of women.

The creation of a liberating community for all men and women.

The promotion of mutuality and harmony.

Feminism is not anti-male.

It is a question that brings to mind some vivid phrases of Maureen Ryan's in a contribution she made to *Search*[4] four years later:

> What we need to ask ourselves is whether that challenge [of refuting idolatry and resisting literal-mindedness in liturgy] deserves to remain buried with the shoulder pads and big hair of the late twentieth century? ... Looking back, I believe we lived through a *kairos* moment, and God forgive us, I think we became confused. I think we sold out for a collar, and I think we missed it, for if our God-images remain unchallenged by contemporary experience, if the metaphors fail to develop, God-talk becomes fossilised.

The problem with trying to make gender issues invisible was epitomised strikingly and in an unexpected way in the eucharist we celebrated to open the Conference in Christ Church Cathedral, Dublin, on the afternoon of Sunday 3 September (though it was entirely predictable, had we thought to predict it).

As mentioned above, I was asked to be the celebrant at this service, the first and only time I was ever invited to celebrate at a major service in the cathedral; Archbishop Walton Empey 'presided' by welcoming the congregation and then generously handed over to me. Others taking part were admirably gender-balanced: the vice principal of the Theological College, William Marshall, read the epistle, Hilary Dungan, recently ordained deacon, read the gospel, the intercessions were led by Susan Green (hospital chaplain, Dublin), Louise Stewart (NSM Connor), and Thea Boyle (lay reader, Dublin); and the preacher was the Archbishop of Armagh, Dr Robin Eames. (Dean John Paterson did not attend.)

---

4. 'Chasing the "old white man": on making the feminine more visible' in *Search – A Church of Ireland Journal*, 27.2., Summer 2004.

Dr Eames, throughout his long and distinguished episcopate, was always known for his diplomatic skills and had justly won much praise for the prayerful and conciliatory manner in which he had presided over the key General Synod debates of 1989 and 1990. He had also achieved worldwide respect for his chairing of the Archbishop of Canterbury's Commission on 'Communion and Women in the Episcopate' in 1988-89.[5] Ever the mediator, he did his very best, as indicated in Chapter Nine above, to get the General Synod of 1991 to 'affirm' as well as to 'note and receive' the bishops' statement that no clergy who objected to the ordination of women should suffer discrimination, loss of respect or lack of preferment in the church on account of their *bona fide* views.[6] Now he had committed himself to addressing the congregation at this conference to celebrate ten years of women's priestly ministry.

He might have been happy to enter into the spirit of the celebration – (he had after all ordained women in Armagh, though not many, and he knew that women had by then more than proved themselves as priests in every diocese of the Church of Ireland) – had it not been that the word 'celebrate' with reference to 'women priests' had caused acute and highly publicised distress to certain members of the long-disbanded 'Concerned Clergy'. John Crawford, in particular, was much quoted in the national newspapers: how could the church *celebrate* a development which had caused such division and dismay? Granted that women clergy might justifiably wish to mark the occasion, surely celebration had to be out of the question?

We had expected that the Primate would be measured and diplomatic in his address. We had not foreseen that he would be so careful of the feelings of our opponents that he would refrain from congratulating or thanking the hard-working women priests present for their years of faithful ministry.

---

5. Lord Eames was later to chair the Lambeth Commission on Communion, 2003-2004, leading to the Windsor Report and its proposal of an Anglican Covenant to address the powder-keg issue of gay clergy, caused by conservative reaction to the election of Gene Robinson as Bishop of New Hampshire in 2003.
6. General Synod, 1991. Motion 3. cf pp 109-111.

These words were the nearest he came to recognising any contribution at all from women clergy:

> The Church of Ireland was the first Anglican Church in these is-
> lands to take the step of opening priesthood and the episcopate to
> women ... a decade ago. Since then women serve in the sacred min-
> istry of the Church of Ireland throughout our various dioceses.
> Inevitably those of you who were ordained in the early days follow-
> ing that decision faced difficulties and pressures. Perceptions and
> curiosity can be unkind as well as sympathetic. I join with you in
> this moment of anniversary as you reflect, give thanks and recom-
> mit yourselves to God's service.
>
> On this occasion as Primate I want to affirm all who serve the
> priesthood of the Church of Ireland. I recognise again as you do that
> there are some who find it hard to accept that women's ordination
> has occurred in the church. I appreciate their feelings and the sincer-
> ity of their views. Sensitivity to those views is just as important as
> our thoughts here tonight as we mark the tenth anniversary of the
> decision of our General Synod.[7]

Later that week I received a hand-written note from the Primate congratulating me on the celebration. I would happily have exchanged it for a public commendation of the 59 women clergy serving in the Church at that time.

The only man to address the Conference as such was Canon Kenneth Kearon, director of the Irish School of Ecumenics, who had served a high profile ministry in the Church of Ireland, as dean of residence in TCD and rector of Tullow, a prosperous parish in south county Dublin.[8] Kearon had always as far as we knew been in favour of women's ordination; his comments as recorded in the report bear out the importance of the question raised above about what might be the distinctive contribution of women clergy to the life of the church:

> The last ten years have been remarkably successful in the accep-
> tance of women's ordination. No one has become an opponent be-
> cause of how women have exercised ministry. Women got stuck in,
> got on with the job, and were just as good as the men. While still a

---

7. Quoted from a script supplied by the Diocesan Information Officer, Dublin, 2000.
8. Kenneth Kearon was to be appointed Secretary General of the Anglican Communion in 2005.

novelty, this aspect will diminish. But some women are willing to play along with that novelty value, for example always wearing a collar. [This comment amused me, since it was not that many years since Ken Kearon had confided to me that it was useful to wear a collar around the parish, so as to be instantly recognisable.]

The novelty and shock value of being a woman priest should not affect the way they operate. Whereas it is necessary to establish the equal validity of women's ministry, an over-strident approach can also be counter-productive. *Having proved that women are as good as men, the question now is how do women shape and change ministry from its male stereotype.* [Italics mine]

The church needs to be more inclusive. This will not happen just because women are ordained … Women are in a unique position to take up the cause for a more inclusive church of the future.[9]

Before the Conference broke up, the participants came up with ten suggested ways that we might celebrate our ten years of priestly ministry and to move forward – to include the serious and the funny, the possible and the impossible. This was the list that emerged from the group sessions:

1. Annual Retreat / Conference
2. Pulpit exchange with parishes who have never experienced a woman priest.
3. Develop a system of mentors or some friends to support each other in ministry.
4. Compile a book of 10 stories of women in ministry – serious and funny.
5. Hug a bloke.
6. Regional support groups.
7. Reach out to those opposed to women's ministry.
8. Encourage those who can't have their vocations recognised.
9. Change the constitution so that the language is inclusive – as has been done in liturgy.
10. Plant a 'Mary Garden'.

Ann Thurston, who had sent the groups off to come up with these suggestions, offered a not dissimilar list of her own:
1. A mentoring system: those already ordained offer to sup-

---

9. *Celebrating 10 Years of Women Priests*, report cited above, p 12.

port the newly ordained or the ordinand. This could be arranged very simply – a 'volunteer system', a list of names – but could be such a help.

2. An annual or bi-annual get-together. This could be just one day perhaps with a single input and otherwise leaving plenty of time to meet and chat and share concerns.

3. Inviting women already ordained to come to the Theological College to talk about their experiences and thus enable the students and the college to reflect on the relationship between theory and practice.

4. Sponsor research on women's experience of priesthood in Ireland.

5. A liaison person with a particular brief to consider gender issues.

6. More women on the staff of the Theological College, perhaps a woman spiritual director.

7. As women opt for the auxiliary [non-stipendiary] ministry it is urgent that this ministry is reviewed and norms and guidelines are put in place. It was very clear from the conference that many women are in very difficult situations.

8. Clergy marriages were not discussed but also need particular consideration – where are the difficulties and strains and the gifts and benefits?

9. Seminars on feminist theology for *male and female* clergy.

10. Gender issues to be part of the agenda for clergy conferences.

Numbers 1 and 2 on Ann's list relate directly to 3 and 1 on the groups' list, so mentoring and an annual conference were high on the common list. However, nothing came of them, as far as I have been able to discover. Numbers 3 and 5 on her list hark back to the WMG, which organised a conference as suggested and had a constant liaison person on the House of Bishops. Again, I don't think anything much was done by way of follow-up.

The question of non-stipendiary clergywomen, whose pain at their 'yellow-pack' status was an underlying theme of the whole conference, surprisingly came up only on Ann's list. The problems they experience and the training they are offered have been much considered down the years, not least by the Commission on Ministry; and it is good that current planning for ministry education will result in a further lessening of the status gap between the paid and unpaid ministry of the church.

What surprised me most in the lists was that there was so little mention of the difficulties experienced by married women clergy, especially mothers of small children, or of problems facing clergy married to one another. There was no mention at all in the groups' list, and Ann's #8 refers to the difficulties almost tangentially. Were participants perhaps nervous about raising the question which had been so much used by opponents to marginalise women's ministry, if not entirely to reject it?

As to research, there *has* been a small amount of this since 2000, but we could do with a lot more. In 2002 David McCready produced an MA thesis for Queen's University Belfast on the ordination of women in the Church of Ireland, a short version of which has been published by the Royal Irish Academy.[10] The full manuscript can be accessed in the Representative Church Body Library. It offers a useful history of the process leading to the ordinations of the first women priests in 1990, which is fair to both sides in the debate, if in need of a few small marginal corrections. This writer referred to it frequently in writing some of the preceding chapters to ensure that nothing of import was omitted. However, the work is strictly historical and offers little in the way of sustained reflection on how the ministry of women might affect the Church of Ireland in the future.

For the General Synod of 2003 the Commission on Ministry published in an appendix to their Report the results of a questionnaire issued in 2002 to women clergy, bishops and archdeacons in the Church of Ireland on the experience of women in the ordained ministry.[11] The research was undertaken by a subcommittee under the chairmanship of the Revd Olive Donohoe, gleaning responses from only 55% of ordained women and 63% of archdeacons, but of every member of the House of Bishops.

---

10. David McCready, 'The Ordination of women in the Church of Ireland', *Proceedings of the Royal Irish Academy*, Vol 106C, 367-394 © 2006 Royal Irish Academy, and for full thesis RCB Library, Thesis 80.
11. Appendix E to the Commission on Ministry Report. *General Synod Reports 2003*, p 369.

The survey looked chiefly at the satisfactions and difficulties of ordained ministry for women, the areas in which women might need more support from church structures, and the extent or lack of freedom – especially for married women – to choose between stipendiary and auxiliary ministry.

The conclusion was that women in the ordained ministry derived great satisfaction from their ministry and that the majority found the pastoral and educational aspect of their ministry the most rewarding. They saw the issues which facilitated or hampered their ministry as being more role-based than gender-based, but nonetheless it was agreed that the difficulty of balancing the demands of family life with ministry fell chiefly on the women. Few had felt discriminated against as women clergy, but in general they observed that the current model and structures of ordained ministry needed to be examined and adjusted to suit the changing context of that ministry.

The report made no recommendations as such, although it had been invited to do so. It gave the last word to one of the episcopal respondents: 'The integrity, quality, and spiritual maturity of the ordained women in the Church of Ireland has made an immense contribution towards changing and changed attitudes towards women in the ordained ministry.'

Another piece of research is Canon Desmond McCreery's thesis completed in 2003, once again for an MA awarded by Queen's University Belfast.[12] Canon McCreery had been one of those who abstained from the vote on women's ordination in 1984, but he subsequently employed three female curates, including Katharine Poulton, the first woman to be ordained in 1987. His aim was to investigate the reception of women clergy in the Church of Ireland by interviewing five male clergy who had played a part in training women clergy in their parishes, five women clergy, and five lay people with experience of women priests at parish level. Though carefully selected, the sample was rather too small to offer conclusive results, but some interesting comments were made, indicative of certain attitudes in the north-east of Ireland at least.

12. W. R. Desmond McCreery, 'An Examination of the ordination of Women after eighteen years in the Church of Ireland', 2003, for Queen's University Belfast MA in Religion and Society. RCB Library, Thesis 94.

Some comments regarding the possible 'inadequacy' of women for the task were somewhat quaint, especially that of the clergyman who considered women had to cope with 'a biological challenge' once a month. Had no one told him that we now have women airline pilots? Or suggested that maybe male hangovers or other self-induced medical conditions can be as debilitating as any female 'biological' condition, or more so?

More seriously, the women clergy interviewed reported various degrees of antagonism or negativity towards their ministry, chiefly from male clergy:

> W1 said that when she ministered overseas she found no antagonism. Here at home W1 was more aware of vibes than overt antagonism. Like W2 she found that much of the antagonism came from extreme or fundamentalist evangelicals. Both these ladies would call themselves evangelical but found that the antagonism emanating from this quarter was sad and hurtful … W3 found no outright antagonism but did detect underlying currents … She once applied to become rector of a country parish and whilst the bishop concerned was pleasant and courteous she heard no more … However, W5 had the most overt antagonism of any of the women. She was shocked by the behaviour of a neighbouring rector who came to celebrate Holy Communion when her own rector was on holiday. He was basically rude and when she presented the bread and wine to him he refused to accept them.[13]

Such incidents, however, are not deeply significant unless they are frequently experienced, and McCreery's interviewees gave no suggestion that this was the case. The comments of the lay people interviewed, however, do give some grounds for concern, though how representative they were of general attitudes, is unclear. As summarised in *Search*:

> Two of the lay people interviewed for this study (L1 and L2) are parochial nominators. L1 admitted that while he would approach the task with an open mind, 'He would probably still be thinking in terms of a male who would have more to offer.' He added that he felt female clergy did not have the ability to carry out the management roles in the parish. L2 would not have a problem with a lady rector *per se*, but might find it more difficult when she was leader of

---

13. McCreery, p 68.

a team of clergy. L4 said that while she would not leave the church over the appointment of a woman rector, she would prefer a man.[14]

McCreery's study also raised the perennial and important question of the compatibility of marriage, motherhood and ordained ministry:

> All the women priests believed there were very real tensions between marriage and ministry … W5 was quite adamant that if she married and had children she would withdraw from ministry for several years and even if she didn't have children she would not allow ministry to affect her relationship with her husband.
>
> W1 suggested the question had to be asked, 'Do women priests really have to do both jobs?' She felt they were simply dancing to the tune of the secular professional women. W2 still finds it difficult, particularly when she has a visiting preacher and has to get home after service to prepare a meal. W3 and W4 are younger women. W3 had children whilst W4 has none. W3 has found it difficult to juggle the roles but agrees it is similar for all professional women … W4 believes the tension is not so much about dichotomy between ministry and marriage but about the way the Church of Ireland has practised the lifestyle of ministry. She says that we are using nineteenth century methods in the twenty-first century. Unsocial hours create huge problems and tensions. Expectations on clergy have changed from both laity and bishops and this has led to cynicism. There is no mechanism for encouragement.[15]

And indeed it is possibly this difficulty women have in 'juggling' marriage and ministry, more than any other factor, which explains the slow development of women's ministry as rectors in the years up to 2003. At this point the figures showed that although the numbers of male and female curates were equal, the percentage of women curates who had proceeded to first rectorships at that point was much lower than that of their male contemporaries.[16] Similarly an unduly large proportion of women had opted for non-stipendiary ministry, making up over 35% of all NSM clergy as against 10% of stipendiaries.

---

14. In 'Female Clergy: Continuing Problems?' by Darren McCallig, *Search* 23.3, Autumn, 2005.

15. McCreery, op. cit. p70-71.

16. McCallig, op. cit. p 252-3; commenting on McCreery, p 105.

Darren McCallig made some acute comments on the situation is his 2005 *Search* article:

Is there some insight to be gained from the fact that employment patterns in the church reflect those in the wider society? Because there too we find women concentrated in part-time posts. Figures for the Republic of Ireland suggest that 70 per cent of part-time or temporary workers are women. The average working week for women is 32.8 hours, as compared with 42 for men. Social commentators point to the lack of subsidised/affordable childcare and the difficulties of juggling work with family life as contributing factors in this regard. Is something similar happening in the church?

And, commenting on one clergywoman's complaint that there were no mechanisms in place for achieving a reasonable balance between ministry and family life:

Isn't it time that we put those mechanisms in place? Is not a minister's marriage and family life as important as their ministry? The view that 'ministry is unique' and 'that ministry is so demanding that marriage and children are bound to suffer', should surely be a cause for alarm rather than the badge of honour it appears to be for some … Could the truth be that women are simply unwilling to allow their family life to suffer in the way that many of their male colleagues may have allowed in the past?

In other words, it is not just women clergy who need more flexible structures to enable healthy family life; male clergy too need to work in a context which respects their family life. This realisation is not exactly new; but maybe it did need the arrival of women on the scene to begin the process of change.

Another piece of research for the same issue of *Search*, which marked fifteen years of women's priesthood in the Church of Ireland, was conducted by the Revd Bernie Daly, former director of pastoral studies at the Theological College, this time specifically on the experience in ministry of full-time women clergy in the Church of Ireland, to all of whom she issued a questionnaire, yielding a response rate of over 75%.[17] While her findings were on the whole positive, showing that most women, including mothers of small children, felt fulfilled and supported in

17 'The Experience of Women as Stipendiary Clergy in the Church of Ireland' by Bernie Daly, *Search* 29.3, Autumn 2005, p 242.

their ministry and considered that their ministry was fully integrated with the rest of their lives, the responses to questions on negativity and sexual harassment or bullying gave cause for concern. She writes:

> Responses showed that 53.5% experienced negativity from male clergy; 34% from male parishioners; 46% from female parishioners. However, almost 75% of negativity was experienced only occasionally, with negligible amounts of frequent or constant negativity reported. Just over half of women (54%) had had their ministry rejected on occasion, specifically because of their gender.
>
> When asked if they had experienced sexual harassment or bullying during training for ministry or after ordination, the response was as follows:
>
> | | |
> |---|---|
> | Sexual harassment in training: | 14.6% |
> | Sexual harassment in ministry: | 21.0% |
> | Bullying in training: | 26.8% |
> | Bullying in ministry: | 43.9% |
> | Who were responsible for these offences? | |
> | Students | 24.4% |
> | Clergy | 41.5% |
> | Parishioners | 19.5% |

These are disturbing statistics. In the space set aside for comments, some women said they felt reluctant to report sexual harassment or bullying as they feared being dismissed as emotional or troublesome. The small number who did report one or other of these issues to a higher authority did not receive any long-standing support, and to the best of their knowledge, the offending behaviour was not addressed.[18]

Nonetheless, almost two-thirds of the respondents felt that their future advancement in the church would not be hindered by their gender – an indication that their negative experiences were fairly isolated and that in general they were well accepted. An overwhelming majority (95%) considered that as women they added a particular dimension to ordained ministry, bringing an overall balance to the whole.

Bernie Daly also had some helpful observations to make on the 'marriage and ministry' question:

---

18. Daly, op. cit., p 244.

A factor that emerges as a result of this survey is that only a small percentage of mothers have sought ordination. Many women may be prevented from doing so because of the present system of training for ministry. For example, women with dependent children, living outside Dublin, must either leave their children at home for five days a week during the academic year or move their entire families to Dublin. The latter solution is often impracticable due to spouses' careers, children's schooling, and the lack of affordable accommodation in Dublin. (This same dilemma also faces married male ordinands who live outside the Dublin area.)

Mothers, who tend to be regarded as the main nurturers in Irish families, may manage to overcome the difficulties encountered in training if they have a good support system. The next hurdle arises after ordination. There is an accepted understanding that a curate or rector of either gender will work a six-day week in addition to some evening engagements. If a married woman is to fulfil this type of commitment she will require a very supportive and flexible spouse, whether or not there are children in the family.

Admitting that the now ongoing restructuring of training requirements will hopefully address this problem, she goes on to suggest that it would be 'heartening if the Church of Ireland could review the current system of appointments,' that is, our structures of ministry.

At present, clergy seeking full-time posts have little choice outside the position of rector or curate. Almost 25% of respondents in this survey chose team ministry as an ideal. No such concept is officially recognised in the Church of Ireland ... but it is a system of ministry which might encourage future female (and male) applicants. Through this system, women could become team rectors or members of a team, as their personal circumstances dictated. The establishment of teams (or area ministry) in which each member, whether full- or part-time, had particular responsibilities, might also help to eliminate the frequent perception that the church fosters a two-tier ordained ministry: stipendiary and non-stipendiary.

Indeed it is the team ministry or collaborative ministry model which seems to be the one towards which the Church of Ireland is ever so slowly inching its way. It has not been pushed in this direction by any concerted demand from female clergy, yet the availability of more women clergy, who are more likely than the men to wish to work part-time, is one of the factors which point to it. The most compelling factor, however, is the continuing amalgamation of rural parishes, requiring huge areas of sparse population to be oversseen by one rector. The availability of more non-stipendiary ministers and lay readers than ever before, the relatively new option of part-time stipendiary ministry, and the move towards providing specific training for different types of lay ministry, all make this increasingly possible.

Nor is the development without a firm theological foundation. The biblical principles of the ministry of all the baptised (for which realistically we should read all the 'practising' Christians of each parish) and the priesthood of the whole people of God would rather seem to demand it.

Looking back twenty-five years to the start of my journey in the Church of Ireland at Kill O' the Grange, I reflect with some nostalgia on how this model was already developing through Billy Gibbons' weekly 7am meetings of his Pastoral Council; how all available gifts for ministry were sought out, enabled and encouraged, and a structure built up in which both lay and clerical ministry was deployed for a variety of responsibilities, delegated and supported by the rector. Over the past twenty years, I have learned just how difficult it is to get such a ministry team to function. It takes an enormous amount of motivation, education and inspiration. In my own parish I tried and failed. With a few exceptions, people were just too embedded in the old model of 'helping the rector' – (and that only when other demands are not unduly pressing) – to accept ongoing responsibility for anything more than the traditional tasks.

Dean Sue Patterson of Killala, writing recently on this subject, outlined two basic models of how to develop the 'collaborative ministry' to which she and many others believe today's church to be called. However we get there, she has no doubts about the principle:

> The shift that is instigated is from viewing ministry as something ordained people do to, for, and often in spite of, lay people, to viewing ministry as something all are baptised into, that we do for and with each other, whether lay or ordained, in order to engage in the church's mission. Where this understanding of ministry is not pre-

sent the result is the diminishment, distortion, and denial of spiritual gifts.[19]

However like me, Sue Patterson is not sure that the pushing of any specific female agenda is the way we move forward into a style of ministry which transcends the old patriarchal, even monarchical, structures. It is more a case of evolution than revolution, and the increasing proportion of women in the ministry, along with the issues raised and possibilities created by their very presence, may be sufficient to start the transformation. In a recent email to me she wrote:

> I see the gender difference as more nuancing my ministry than bringing something qualitatively different. And that nuancing is the product of a three-way interaction between people's habitual ways of relating to women, their expectations of clergy (or clergy+ spouse), and my particular gifts, strengths and weaknesses ... If you are looking for a statement of principle, I would say that I do not believe that being a woman should be the focus of one's ministry. It is the thing one works through in realising a vision of ministry that is above and beyond gender issues – 'in Christ there is neither male nor female'.

We agreed that our gender will shape our vision in various ways but it should not determine or obstruct it. Like her, I am more and more inclined to think it is healthy that women here have generally just got on with the job and haven't gone self-consciously political about gender issues.

All the same, Sue Patterson does feel that women are inclined to have the edge over men in terms of developing fresh styles of ministry, finding creative ways of working together to develop alternative ministry structures within or around the traditional one. So it is arguable that as women clergy we should at least be on the alert and willing to push for new structures as well as increased flexibility. That said, we must guard against stereotyping men as overly structure-bound, competitive loners. Some may be; many are not.

* * *

_____

19. 'Developing Collaborative Ministry' in Search 30.2, Summer 2007, p 115.

S O HAVING RAISED THE QUESTION of how we as women might seek to transform a style of ministry which is no longer suitable for today's church in today's world, and having challenged myself and my female clergy colleagues further by quoting Kenneth Kearon's suggestion that we are in a unique position to take up the cause for a more inclusive church of the future, I find myself somewhat uneasy about the burden of responsibility such challenges seem to lay on us. Yet neither should we shirk the tasks God has prepared for us to do.

I am very proud of the women clergy of the Church of Ireland. My observation is that they have shown great courage, adaptability, devotion to God and God's flock, and that they have demonstrated undeniable gifts for preaching, teaching, leadership and pastoral care. Each woman has used to the best of her ability the particular gifts God has given her for her calling. It is perhaps a little disappointing that, while some women have been considered for episcopal election, no woman bishop has been consecrated as yet; but I could not point to any bishop elected in recent years who might with advantage have ceded his place to a woman. I have no doubt that a woman will be elected when the time, and the call, is right, without any need for positive discrimination or any resort to tokenism.

Faithfulness to our call is the essential thing, not climbing the ladder of privilege and power. If we and those who come after us can simply continue to respond to our call, always being true to ourselves and the leading of God's Spirit, I believe that the God who called us all will lead us, along with our brothers and sisters in the whole Church, into the ministry he desires. We have only to be faithful and watchful, caring and courageous. Amen. So be it.

APPENDIX I

Church of Ireland Women's Ministry Group

QUESTIONS ON CONDITIONS AND DEPLOYMENT OF ORDAINED WOMEN

1. Are you married   single   widowed

2. Your age range: Under 30   30-45   45-60   over 60

3. If married, is your husband:
>   ordained
>   in employment tied to location
>   self-employed or in locationally flexible employment
>   unemployed or retired

4. How many children have you
>   under school age
>   school age

5. Are you currently working

FULL TIME   PART TIME   ON LEAVE   AUXILIARY

Please give indication of hours per week:

6. If applicable, how much time did you/would you hope to take off for the birth and full-time nurture of each child, and for how long did/would you work only part-time to gain extra family time? (Please specify if leave was paid or unpaid.)

ON LEAVE   PART TIME WORK
>   3 months or less
>   3-6 months
>   6-12 months
>   between 1 and 3 years
>   between 3 and 5 years

7. Did your husband take time off for the same purpose? If so, please specify time on schedule above.

8. Was the diocesan administration supportive of you in arrangement for your leave and/or part-time work?

VERY   FAIRLY   NOT VERY   NO

Please specify anything particularly noteworthy.

9. Has a change in your husband's job location necessitated change in your own parish employment?

YES   NO   NEARLY

10. Was or is your re-entry to full-time ministry difficult to arrange?

VERY   FAIRLY   NOT VERY   NO

Please give details:

11. How many hours do you normally devote to parish work weekly?

UNDER 30   30 – 40   40 – 50   OVER 50

12. Have your hours spent on parish work decreased due to family needs?

YES   NO

13. Have your husband's working hours decreased for the same reason?

YES   NO

14. Have there been any serious complaints on this score:
Re yourself?   Re your husband?

15. Do you take a regular day off from parish duties with your family?

YES   SOMETIMES   NO

16. Do you find your parish supportive of your need for family time?

VERY   FAIRLY   NOT VERY   NO

17. Do your parishioners give practical help to release you from routine child care or domestic work for your parish duties?

REGULARLY   OCCASIONALLY   NO

18. If not, how do you manage?

19 Do you feel that a new pattern of Christian family life is evolving, which you are in some sense modelling for your congregation? Please comment:

20. How do you feel that church structures could best be adjusted to further the fullest and most effective participation of ordained women?

21. What development have you seen in the attitudes of a) men and b) women in your parish to women, and particularly married women, clergy?

22. Any further comments?

APPENDIX II

Summary of Suggestions submitted to Select Committee on Women's Ordination by the Women's Ministry Group along with results of their research on the conditions of married women clergy in the Anglican Communion for General Synod 1990.

Suggestions arising from our research, and from our personal experience in Ireland, are as follows:

i) Flexibility in addressing administrative problems occasioned by women priests and deacons will be essential in the initial phase.

ii) Pastoral support for women clergy and their husbands and families is of high importance. The appointment of women deans or chaplains for women's ministry in each province, and before long in each diocese, would be helpful – both for the pastoral care of clergywomen and for communication with diocesan and church authorities.

iii) A new category of part-time stipendiary ministry should be introduced to maximise the ministerial contribution of mothers of young families.

iv) More flexible training structures are needed for mothers of young families – and arguably for some fathers also.

v) Women should not be limited permanently to n.s.m. work on account of initial shortage of time for family reasons.

vi) Conditions for clergy couples should be carefully considered, with due regard to the fostering of their family life. A couple who between them do more work than one cleric could reasonably be expected to do should not be expected to live on one stipend.

vii) Pension arrangements will need to take account of spells of part-time or n.s.m. work and possibly a lifetime of shared ministry.

viii) A larger pool of auxiliary or peripatetic clergy may be needed, if sufficient retired clergy are not available.

ix) If the ordination of women to the priesthood were to be delayed, it would be important to affirm the appointment of deacons-in-charge and to recognise senior deacons' right to officiate at marriages.

x) We note that other churches, including the Church of England, appoint women as area or rural deans, canons, directors of ordinands etc. and that churches which priest women appoint them also as archdeacons, cathedral deans etc. As more women are ordained in Ireland, it will be important to use them in this way here also.

xi) We are aware of the importance of the pastoral care of those who find it difficult to accept the idea of women in the priesthood or episcopate. While it is important that no one be obliged personally to accept the ministry of a woman priest, or indeed of any priest, and that bishops' rights not to ordain women be respected in the initial phase, we would nonetheless suggest that any actual 'no go areas' for women priests in the Church of Ireland would be divisive and counter-productive.

Submitted 23 November 1989

Women clergy in the Church of Ireland 2008*

Deans
Sue Patterson, 1988, I Kilmoremoy, Killala, 2004, Dean Killala, 2005.

Rectors
Janice Aiton , 2001, I Dunboyne and Rathmolyon, 2004
Frances Bach, 1994, I Armoy, Connor, 2000.
Denise Cadoo, 1995, I Gilford, Dromore, 2006
Louise Crawford, 2002, I Aghadowey, Derry, 2005
Eileen Cremin, 1988, I Fermoy 2006
Olive Donohoe, 1995, I Mountmellick, Kildare 1998.
Hilary Dungan, 2000, I Maryborough, Leighlin, 2003.
Stella Durand, 2000, I Kiltegan, Leighlin, 2003
Barbara Fryday, 1992, Canon, Ossory 2003; I Clonmel (St Mary), Lismore, 2007.
Nancy Gillespie, 1997, I Stradbally, Leighlin, 2000; Canon, Ossory, 2006.
Sonia Gyles, 2001, I. Sandford, Dublin, 2004.
Sandra Hales, 2002, I Celbridge, Glendalough, 2006.
Elizabeth Hanna, 2001, I. Magherally, Dromore, 2004.
Olive Henderson, 1997, I Rathdrum, Glendalough, 2007.
Judith Hubbard-Jones, 1987, I Kinneigh, Cork, 2002.
Maria Jansson, 2001, I Wexford, Ferns, 2004.
Stella Jones (formerly Mikhail), 2002, I Clonenagh, Ossory, 2005.
Rosemary Logue, 1993, I Sixmilecross, Armagh, 2005.
Eithne Lynch, 1997, I Kilmoe, Cork 2001
Dorothy McVeigh, 1993, I Annaghmore, Armagh, 2004.
Mercia Malcolm, 1987, I Carnmoney, Connor, 2003
Ruth Murray, 2003, I Woodschapel, Armagh, 2006.
Lynda Peilow, 1997, I Clonsast, Kildare, 2001.

* The first date fater each name is the date of ordination to the dia-conate; the second is the date of appointment to the current position.

Sandra Pragnell, 2001, I Dundalk, 2005.

Donna Quigley, 2001, I Derryvolgie, Connor, 2004.

Marie Rowley-Brooke, 2002, I Nenagh Union, Killaloe, 2005.

Kathy Southerton, 1992, I Tubbercurry, Achonry, 2004.

Pat Storey, 1997, I Londonderry St Augustine, Derry, 2004.

Gillian Wharton, 1993, I Booterstown, Dublin, 2004.

Olivia Williams, 2001, I Carlow, Leighlin, 2005.

Bishops' Curates and vicars

Janet Catterall, 1987, BC Mostrim, Ardagh, 2002, Canon St
    Patrick's Dublin, 2005.

Irene Lyttle, 2001, BC Leckpatrick, Derry, 2007.

Katharine Poulton, 1987, St George and St Thomas, Dublin,
    2000, Canon CCC Dublin, 2007.

Edith Quirey, 2001, BC Belfast St Stephens, Connor, 2007.

Helene Tarneberg-Steed, 1996, Dean's V Cork, 2004.

Gill Withers, 1997, V Knock, Down, 2005.

Special ministries

Grace Clunie, 1995, Director of Celtic Spirituality, Armagh,
    2007.

Susan Green, 1992, Chaplain Adelaide and Meath Hospital,
    2000.

Patricia Hanna, 1999 Chaplain Univ of Limerick, Killaloe, 2007.

Pat Mollan, 1997, Dep Dir CMH, Downpatrick, Down, 2004.

Anne Taylor, 1994, Children's Ministry Officer, Dublin, 2005.

Sheila Zietsman, 1990, Chaplain, East Glendalough School,
    Glendalough, 1996.

Curates

Denise Acheson, 2005, C Ballyholme, Down, 2005.

Amanda Adams, 2006, C Ballymena, Connor, 2006.

Clare Ashbridge, 2007, C Donachcloney, Dromore, 2007.

Jennifer Bell, 2004, C Belfast St Nicholas, Connor, 2006.

Elaine Dunne , 2005, C Castleknock, 2005.

Gunilla Aquilon-Elmqvist, 1991, C.Wexford, Ferns, 2005.

Jane Galbraith, 1995, C Limerick 2003.

Adrienne Galligan, 2003, C Seapatrick, Dromore 2003.

Isobel Jackson, 2004, C Lismore (Stradbally) Lismore 2005.

Ruth Jackson, 2002, C Carrigrohane, Cork 2005.
Diane Matchett, 2005, C. Lisburn Christ Church, Connor, 2005.
Joanne Megarrell, 2003, C Moira, Dromore, 2003.
Jacqueline Mould, 1991, C. Belvoir, Down, 2003.
Elaine Murray, 2005, C. Kilkenny, Ossory, 2005.
Elaine O'Brien, 1997, C Clogherny, Armagh, 2006.
Joyce Rankin, 2003, C St Ann and St Stephen, Dublin. 2003.
Patricia Taylor, 2005, C Wicklow, Glendalough, 2005.

Priests in charge
Moreen Hutchinson, 2001, P in C Ardclinis, Connor, 2004.
Lynne Rogers, 2003, P in C New Ross, 2007.
Susan Watterson, 1987, P in C Killarney, Ardfert and Aghadoe, 2007.

NSMs
Eileen Armstrong, 1995, Navan, Meath.
Avril Bennett, 2000, Lucan, Glendalough.
Doris Clements, 1995, Killala, Tuam, Canon, Achonry, 2005.
Jenny Crowley, 2003, New Ross, Ferns.
Janice Elsdon, 1995, South Belfast, Connor.
Edith Ferguson, 2002, Bandon, Cork.
Paula Geary, 2006, Moviddy Union, Cork.
Ruth Gill, 2004, Birr, Killaloe.
Martha Gray-Stack, 1990, Chaplain Kingston College, Cloyne.
Carol Harvey, 2006, Carnmoney, Connor.
Elizabeth Henderson, 1999, Finaghy, Connor.
Shiela Johnson, 1996 Clondevaddock, Raphoe.
Anita Kerr, 2007, Sligo, Elphin.
Avril Kingston, 1994, Waterford.
Sandra Lindsay, 1993, Roscommon, Elphin.
Katie McAteer, 2006, Conwal, Raphoe.
Norma McMaster, 2004, Holmpatrick, Dublin.
Hazel Minion, 2003, Douglas, Cork.
Joyce Moore, 2001, Drogheda, Armagh.
Bobbie Moore, 2006, Drung, Kilmore.
Isobel Nixon, 1994, Clogher.
Margaret Pringle, 2005, Clogher Cathedral, Clogher.
Lesley Robinson, 2002, Roscrea, Killaloe.

Maureen Ryan, 1998, Canon St Patrick's Dublin, 2000, Tuam,
    2005, Galway, Tuam
Hazel Scully, 2001, Chap. Wilson's Hos., 2006.
Alison Seymour-Whitely, 2007, Clogher.
Aisling Shine, 2003, Clondalkin, Dublin.
Alice Stewart, 2000, Cloughfern, Connor.
Louise Stewart, 2000, Malone, Connor.
Margaret Sykes, 2006, Ardamine, Ferns.
Elizabeth Thompson, 2006, Rossorry, Clogher.
Marie Sylvia Walshe, 1999, Down.
Cecily West, 1994, Dublin.
Janet White-Spunner, 1994, Shinrone, Killaloe.
Tanya Woods, 2002, Bailieborough, Kilmore.
Jean Wynne, 2002, Mullingar, Meath.

Retired stipendiary
Kathleen Brown (formerly Young) 1988, I Belfast St Paul,
    Connor, 1992, Canon St Anne's Belfast, 2000, R 2007.
Bronwen Carling, 1991, Cashel, R 2001.
Bernie Daly, 1997, formerly Lecturer in Pastoralia CITC and C
    Taney, Dublin. R 2006.
Elizabeth Johnston, 1981 (CNI), BC Ballymacarret St Christopher,
        Down, 1993; Canon Down, 2001. R 2003.
Ginnie Kennerley, 1988, I Narraghmore 1993, Canon CCC
    Dublin 1996, R 2005.
Liz McElhinney, 1997, I Calry, Elphin 2001. R 2007).
Hilary Wakeman, 1987, Hon canon, Norwich 1994-6, I Kilmoe,
    Cork 1996. R 2001.
Ann Wooderson, 1989, I Celbridge, 1989, 2006.

Retired or semi-retired NSMs
Olive Boothman, 1994, Clondalkin, Dublin, R 2005.
Margaret Gilbert, 1992, Drumcondra, Dublin, R 2007.
Ann Wallace, 1995, Abbeyleix, Leighlin, R 2007.

Other occupation with permission to officiate
Nicola Harvey-Neill, 1995, Limerick.

Note on part-time ministries
There has been an increased flexibility in C of I structures, allow-ing for part-time paid ministry. Special ministries, bishops cura-cies and positions as priests in charge of a parish offer such posi-tions most easily, but many in such positions work full-time. NSMs by definition work part-time without pay, though occa-sionally they have opted into full-time or half-time work with expenses and residence provided.

Index